I Hate Social Networking

Other Books by Ebony Williams:
A Crooked Smile
The Single Chronicles Part 1

I Hate Social Networking
Ebony Williams

Copyright © 2014 by Ebony Williams

ISBN: 978-1-312-22837-5

Cover design by: Bawd Designs

Printed in the United States of America

"The lord is my light and my salvation so why should I be afraid? The lord is my fortress protecting me from danger so why should I tremble? When evil people come to devour me, when my enemies and foes attack me they will stumble and fall. Though a mighty army surrounds me my heart will not be afraid even if I am attacked. I will remain confident,"

PSALM 27 1-3

Dear Diary,

Is it just me, or are Facebook, MySpace, Tagged and whatever other time-wasting, soul-sucking, mind-boggling bs networking sites full of lames? Facebook is the QUEEN of "Tough Guys"; MySpace is dead, but where everyone is a musician; and Tagged is where perverts can peep you out. All these sites give men interweb balls filled with words of testosterone. Females swear they are models by posting a bathroom picture and little boys replace their display pic with one that looks nothing like them. All these sites are making it easier for enemies to become your best friend. Guys can brag on how much money they make, and females can stalk their exes. What happened to "Hey, wanna get a coffee?" Since when did that turn into "What's your Instagram name?" I miss the romance of talking on the phone for hours; now it's been replaced by texting and Facebook poking. If you ask me, this blows. I want LOVE, PEOPLE! Is that too much to ask? Well, enough of the venting for now, time to get some shuteye before work.

<3 I Need Stability Hope

* * *

Now I know you're wondering, "How and why does Hope [me] hate social networking?" Well, ladies and gents, sit tight; this will be a bumpy ride.

Hi, my name is Hope. I'm 32; have a great job; family, check; friends, oh yeah, check; money, meh, it's so-so, could be better; a man...yeah, that's a big fat negative.

Why? Well I used to have one—a man, a boo-thang, whatever ya'll want to call it. We were together for six years. Everything was perfect until we almost hit the seven-year mark. Then we tragically ended like Brad and Jen, Ryan and Reese, and Demi and Ashton. No, I am not crazy for comparing my relationship to celebrities' because…well, I'm not. Long story short: It was a horrible, emotional and yet comical situation. (Don't worry—details to come later!) After that lovely relationship, my friends and family tried their best to dig me out of my hole and wanted so desperately for me to begin my life on a site called Bang. My cousin said, "Bang is where you can find your soul mate." May I mention he hasn't found one? My sister said, "It's where the freaks come out at all times of the day," which is true, and so why should I waste my time?

Even though I fought, cried, begged and pleaded to not be thrown into the lion's den of the social networking world, they did the exact opposite. How fitting, huh?

Well, enough of the jibber-jabber; let's meet some people, shall we?! Who do you want to meet first? My Betty Crocker mom; sports-loving dad; psychotic-but-loving married sister; or how about my dysfunctional, delusional, but loving friends? Well, since I gave you a choice and you didn't respond, we will start off with Hanky the ex.

Hanky
(No, not the Christmas poo.)

He stands tall at about five-foot-five. His face is pale, but may I say, he's Mexican. And why his parents named him Hanky? I have no friggin' clue. He was sweet. We understood each other well, considering the language barrier, and he could make the best tacos in the world. He said it was the meat. He didn't use ground beef. Instead— Wait, sorry. Off subject. Back to Hanky.

We met in 2009. I was running, and he was walking with his niece. I had my iPod on full-blast, running to my favorite song, "Boom Boom Pow" by the Black Eyed Peas, and soon enough, right when I turned the corner of 6th and Era, I Boom-boom-powed right into his niece. That's right; I took out his six-year-old niece instead of him. I like to think that our first date was us riding in the back of an ambulance, making intense eye contact as they hooked his niece up to a respirator. Soon we were at the hospital and the medics were taking his niece into the ER. Hanky went through, but we never broke eye contact until the door shut. I waited in the lobby for what seemed like a decade. Five minutes after the solid black doors shut, Hanky came out and said, "She will

1

be okay." He turned right around and walked back to the room. There I was, standing alone in a hospital lobby, wondering about the strange man that had captured my heart.

Every day for the next two weeks I jogged the same route, hoping to run into him again. I finally gave up and decided to get a coffee at Lila's Coffee House. I was sent by my evil boss to get her usual 12-calorie coffee, no sugar, no cream, hold the cup. Having my hands full, I was backing into the doorway to leave the shop when I heard a sudden thud. People around me gasped and others said, "Is she okay?" I looked through my dimmed Dolce & Gabbana sunglasses and couldn't believe what I saw. There he was—Hanky—and there she was—Rosa, his niece—on the ground yet again because of me.

Soon the ambulance pulled up and the medic jumped out. "Are you kidding me? You two again? Seriously! This poor little girl!" said the medic.

"Hey, it's not my fault! She should wear a bell!" I replied.

"Well, she had one, but she lost it," said Hanky.

"You guys are horrible people; I hope she doesn't have a concussion this time."

We all hopped into the ambulance, and Hanky and I took another romantic ride to the hospital. Now, you can't tell me this isn't destiny. So there he was, my knight in shining armor, Mr. Steal My Heart. I had to come up with conversation! Come on, Hope, think!

"Hey, so I'm sorry for hitting your daughter again." Fishing is always good.

"Oh, it's okay."

"So, she is your daughter? Tell your wife I say sorry."

"No wife, and no, she's my niece."

With those magic words I was instantly in love. We locked eyes again all the way to the hospital. Nurses and doctors were looking at us as if we were crazy. Our eye contact was broken yet again by the black doors. Hanky came out and said that she had a concussion so he'd be there for a while. He turned around and was about to go through the double doors.

"Wait, what's your name?" I asked.

"Hanky."

"Like the Christmas poo?"

"No, like Hanky."

"Well, hi, I'm Hope."

"Okay. Well, nice seeing you again. Too bad it's because of my niece."

"Hope she gets better."

We ended up talking for fifteen minutes, and in those

fifteen minutes I thought I was in heaven. We exchanged numbers and our blissful romance began. We started off texting for days on end and then moved to long conversations on the phone. Which, if you ask me, is amazing because talking on the phone is a lost art nowadays.

Our first date was at a place called Spice, which is one of Tuscan's most infamous vegan sushi and barbeque pits. They had an amazing sounding menu, but surprisingly, vegan sushi barbeque pit doesn't taste as good as it may seem. We both ended up getting food poisoning and stayed cuddled up for an amazing four days. Between the naps, throw-ups, and force-feeding, Hanky and I started to fall in love.

After our fabulous week together of getting healthy, Hanky and I continued dating for a couple more months before things really started to get serious. Years started to go by, and in my head I was planning a wedding, picking baby names, and looking at houses to buy. Life seemed amazing!

Before we knew it, we were going into our six-year anniversary, and he'd already moved in. Then Hanky lost his job and became depressed, and he lived on my couch and not in my bedroom.

It seemed like everything was turning into a fight with Hanky: if I asked him what he wanted for breakfast or if he wanted to see a movie, or even if I just said, "Hey, babe, I love you." The slightest movements, words, and whatever else you can think of would set my little love monkey off and leave me crying or headed to kickboxing class. I'm sorry, I know he's being a shit right now, but I thought PMS was *my* thing?

We slowly became roommates instead of lovers. Our conversation started to die, and his love for *Call of Duty* and *Twilight* sparked some heated arguments. One night I sat back at the dinner table, staring at him across the way. He was reading the newest issue of *Cosmopolitan* and giggling. He would put the magazine down, eat, look at me, then giggle again and keep reading. After about four times of this foolery, I finally asked, "What's so funny?"

"They say there's more than fifty sex positions."

"Okay, and?"

"I've only seen three."

Oh, no, he didn't! Did he just say that? To my face? Well, Mr. No-Job, Belly-Fat, *Call-of-Duty*-Playing Jerk-Tard, if you were sexy then I might show you more than three! Did I say this? No, just in my head, and I brushed it off.

He then began to read another story and laughed even harder. Now here I am, trying to do research and enjoy my freakin' bowl of Captain Crunch, but I CAN'T!

"Okay, Hanks, dear, honey pot, what's so funny now?"

"Oh you wouldn't get it," he said, shrugging me off.

"Really? You're reading a magazine aimed at women, so try me."

"Okay, okay. Well, it says here that when we women get into relationships and get comfy, then we start to gain weight and be extra emotional and sometimes unbearable."

"Okay, and?"

"Well, all that applies to you, EXCEPT they forgot to add smelly!"

As Hanky sat at the table dying of laughter, I slowly pulled off my glasses, got up from the table, started laughing, and walked to the back room. He soon followed me, watching as I packed a suitcase, and asked if I was taking a trip. I kept laughing and continued to grab clothes and throw them into the bag as neatly as I could.

"Wait a minute," he said, looking puzzled and a little confused with a Cheerio stuck to his mouth. "That's my stuff." I smiled and kept laughing at him. "Where are we going?" I continued to laugh and slammed more stuff into the boxes I grabbed out of the closet.

"We aren't going anywhere. You are sloppy Joe."

"Who's Joe?"

"Today you are, and I'm done cleaning up your mess!"

"I lost my job and I'm depressed and—"

"And you're now out of a home."

"REALLY?! Thanks, Jen!"

"Who's Jen?"

"Or should I call you Demi, or how about Reese!"

"What the hell are you talking about?!"

"We reached our seven-year mark like they did! So now I'm Brad, Ashton, and Ryan!"

"Alright! STOP READING *COSMO*, YOU TARD! And for the record, Demi and Ashton are still together!"

"Not according to *Us Weekly*! It's been MONTHS since they've been together! He's now banging Mila, you know, Jackie from *That '70s Show*?"

He pulled the magazine out from what seemed to be his pants. I continued to pack his crap, placing it not-so-nicely outside, along with him. There he was, looking sad and lonely, so I slammed the door.

Now look at me! Am I sure I want to do this? Six years, and I'm choosing to throw it away because of selfish reasons?

Since I couldn't answer my questions right away, I

went to the fridge and grabbed my big tub of Chunky Monkey ice cream. I cried while watching *Dirty Dancing*, reciting the line, "No one puts baby in the corner " My phone rang for hours, days, weeks and almost months. I didn't answer. I was in complete solitude.

* * *

Dear Diary,

  So, six years wasted, huh? Well, I guess I'll just have you and ice cream forever! Well maybe not ice cream because I am lactose intolerant, but anyways my depression starts now.

<3 Fuck Life I Don't Know What I'm Doing Hop

Wakey, Wakey, No Crying over Hanky

After years of being with him, I finally called it quits. I stopped crying after three months and went back to the gym to work off Mr. Chunky Monkey. Walking into Sexy Time, aka the cheapest gym membership in Arizona, I felt right at home. On the treadmill was a fat lady eating chips, on the bike an old man with neon knee-high socks, and then I was greeted by the middle-aged man who was slowly balding and had his shirt tucked into his shorts, which were pulled up way too high.

"Hey! Welcome to Sexy Time, what's your membership number?"

"Yeah, hi, it's three, four, five, four, five, six."

"Wow, you have a great memory, that's hot. Usually people will look at their keychain. You must have some type of powers besides being hot."

"Yeah, no, it's just an easy number."

"True, you're funny. I'm good at memorizing numbers too; maybe if you give me yours I can show you how fast I can memorize it."

As Ted—according to his nametag—continued to stare, chew his gum loudly, and smile, I kinda sorta threw up

9

in my mouth. I tried to be nice and see if Mr. Awkward was going to say anything else, but when he didn't I grabbed my stuff and speed walked back to the locker room.

Looking back as if someone were following me, I sat quickly on the bench, rested my head on the locker, and opened my eyes. I soon realized I was in a pool of out-of-shape women who really didn't care. They were walking around naked or half-naked, eating, talking amongst each other, and giggling. Yup, I was right at home. I took my belt off and let my chunky monkey hang out freely. After sharing a bag of Doritos with my new friend Olga, dishing on my ex and crying into her elbow fat, I decided to make my way towards the treadmill and make it my bitch.

Throwing my sporty towel over my shoulder and walking out of the locker room like I owned this gym made me feel like a badass. I jumped on the treadmill and started to speed walk, pumping my arms and taking deep breaths. Soon enough some slim tramp stamp came on the treadmill right next to me. WHY?! There were 10 others that were WIDE open! Does this happen to anyone else besides me? Trampy smiled and jumped on the treadmill, perky as can be with her matching tank, shorts, and shoelaces. I was walking at a brisk 3.2 and she had the nerve to speed up to 5.7. Slowly jogging, she looked over to me in disgust with a fake smile. *So now*

Ms. Trampy wants to compete, huh? Well I'm down. I then hit my speed to 5.7 and she moved hers to 6.8. Thinking this was a test and God wanted me to own this bitch, I met her challenge and went to 6.8. Before I knew it we were running at a full-out sprint at 11.0 on the treadmill. Those poor machines smelled of burning rubber and hair. Why hair? Well, we both ate it and passed out, leaving our precious locks to get stuck.

After being rescued by some hot men in the medical field, I had to check out of the hospital and pay an ass-kicking amount of co-pay. LAME! I looked in the mirror and saw my badly damaged hair. Oh well, off to the salon I went!

Being cheap, I decided to step into Hot Cutz. It was a nice salon, just off the highway next to a flea market and a gas station, advertising five-dollar hair cuts. I'm not one to complain. I walked in and got seated immediately. Soon I was greeted by a man named John "Scissor Hands." He was the best at the salon! Excited to have a haircut by the number one man in there, I felt like a bad ass.

"Come, come, sit, my love! Oh, what do we have here? No, no, no! What happened?"

"Hey, I'm Hope, and I ran on the treadmill."

"Ummm explain, honey."

"This blond tramp tried to outrun me and I accepted

her challenge. Long story short, we passed out and my hair got caught in the, you know, treadmill thingy."

Staring at me like I was the stupidest person alive, he smiled, laughed, and turned my chair around. "Don't worry, honey, John will take care of you." He flapped the draping around my neck and began to cut. *Snip, snip, chop, chop*, was all I heard for about 10 minutes, and then BAM, I was done. He dusted me off and spun me around.

"Voilà! What do you think?"

I looked up with so much excitement! Then I saw myself. I looked like a lesbian. Not the cute kind, the butch kind. My haircut looked worse than Justin Bieber's, Lance Bass's, and Miley Cyrus's combined! I screamed and ran out, not paying my five dollars.

I locked myself in my house, not budging for the rest of the day. Instead I looked in the mirror, figuring out how to deal with this mess on my head. The next day I was supposed to go back to work; I was definitely not excited. That night I was headed to bed early.

I wished I'd taken more time off because my boss, Ms. Perfect, was riding my ass, and I mean hard! I slipped into the office and I knew no one saw me. I did the army crawl past the receptionist, tuck-and-rolled it passed the glass meeting room, then shimmied along the cubical walls of my coworkers to get to my desk. I finally reached my destination, sat down, and took a breath. I looked to my right and saw the picture of me and ass face. I smiled for a second, reminiscing about the memories, then threw it in the trash. After working away for about 10 minutes, I got up and went to the water dispenser. Right when I bent down to grab a drink, BAM! There she was. Ms. Perfect.

"S'up, Hope?"

"Um, hi, Kelly"

"So, over the heartache yet?"

"Yup."

"Well, besides looking like a total lesbian," she said as she flipped her golden blond hair in my face, knocking down my water, "I'm sorry to hear that you and Steve—"

"Hanky."

"Yeah, Frankfort broke up. That's really sad. You know I'm a real romantic."

Sure she was. She'd never been in a relationship that lasted more than 45 minutes.

"Well, thanks."

"Maybe you need to be pretty."

"Excuse me?"

"Yeah, be pretty, Ya know, get one of those surgeries on your face to snip here and there, then a lil' something to

13

snip and tuck everything else. Oh yeah, and get a nice weave, you know, extensions. No straight guy wants a lesbian-looking GF. Well, gotta go to a meeting. I'll talk to you later!"

I hate her face, her boobs, and everything else about her. I know what you're thinking: How did dingbat get this job? Well, her daddy owns the company, and his son Matt is as flamboyantly gay as one can be. I mean, he's a real flamer! But he's smarter than Malibu Bimbo. Matt has an education, is good looking, knows the business, and is great with math. Kelly, on the other hand, sleeps her way into clients' pockets.

Plus, I don't see why she was in such a rush; we both were going to the same meeting! I hate the fact that my boss forgets that I'm her assistant.

A few minutes after Kelly walked in the room, I followed behind with her 12-calorie coffee. Say it with me: "the twelve-calorie, no-sugar, no-cream, hold-the-cup coffee." How am I supposed to bring this beezy her coffee with no cup? And she looks at me every time with that stupid *Whaaat?* face. Did I mention that I hate this chick?

I work in one of the most competitive fields, and trust me, some days at the office can be cutthroat! Who do I work for? Sharps. Now, I know you probably don't know what that is. Some might think it's a knife company, but I work for one of the most prestigious pen-making companies in the world! Well, okay, I over exaggerated; it's the biggest pen company in Arizona. DON'T JUDGE! Everyone uses pens! Anyway, as Kelly was speaking, I couldn't help but replace her face with one belonging to Chewbacca and also substituting her voice with Sean Connery's. Every time I do this it makes the meetings go by so much faster.

"Good morning, my sexy staff!"

Really? Did she just called us sexy? This is what I was looking at in the meeting room: So we have Beth, who is very overweight and smells like ketchup and feathers; then we have Steve, who smells pens and has humongous glasses; may I mention Alan, who has Tourette's; Sean, who's Mexican and doesn't speak English; Stacey, who licks stamps; Melanie, who is Kelly's best friend, a brunette bimbo; and of course her brother Matt, the flamingo color-wearing flamer who has every ascot in any color imaginable... oh, and he wears bangles.

"So, sexies! Want to know what we are gonna talk about today? Drum roll, please..." Ugh, Kelly was getting on my nerves with her overly bouncy boobs and hair flipping this early in the morning. What was this chick on? She proceeded to look towards Steve, who hit the desk once for her drum roll.

"BUDGET CUTS!" Everyone looked around, wondering why this was such exciting news to her.

"What do you mean?" asked Beth.

"I mean, someone will be FIRED toooooday!"

"How is that song-worthy?" asked Steve.

"Well, drum roll, and I will tell you how and who will be cut."

"NO! No more damn drum rolls, Kelly, just tell us who will be cut!" I demanded. *Yeah, that's right, beezy, you better respect my authority and tell me.*

"Alright, alright. Geez, everyone is so uptight! So we will be cutting...MATT!" Everyone gasped and zoned in on Matt. Kelly was now the bitchiest, most deceitful female on the face of this earth. I mean, who cuts their own brother from the family company?

Matt laughed as he played with his colorful ascot. He stood up and made his way towards Kelly.

"You're cutting me?"

"Yes, broham, I am"

"What the flying frickers!"

"Yeah, I know this must be tough on you, but you're not up to par with this company."

"What? I know more about Sharps than you ever will,

you plastic, bleached tramp!"

"Awww, look, everyone, Matt is getting a little upset! Hey, flame-tard, Daddy left me in charge not you."

"Yes, I am aware, and I hope you know that you're getting old and your lady parts won't seal deals like they used to."

"Then I will use the money I make here to snip and tuck, baby, snip and t-u-c-k!"

"Aww, look, everyone, bimbo whore can spell!"

Soon they began screaming, scratching and wind milling towards each other. The floor was covered with Jessica Simpson extensions and colorful ascots. About five minutes into the fight we decided to call security only because it started to get pretty sad. Matt was screaming, "I hate your perfect face!" and Kelly was screaming, "I know, it is perfect, huh?" Then they both started to cry. Now that was a scene that no one wanted to see.

So after that ridiculous meeting, Kelly skipped to her office with her minion Melanie following close behind. They sat in her office laughing, placing Kelly's extensions back in her hair and fixing her makeup. All this drama and crying and it was only 10 a.m.; we had seven more hours left. *Sweet baby Jesus, can you please help me keep my sanity for the rest of the day?*

* * *

Alright, so, diary, today was a very redonk day. Big Tits Magee decided to can her own brother and tell me that I need to be prettier. I just got out of my slump from ass face and I find myself looking pretty damn hot (despite my haircut). Granted, I was wearing an oversized cardigan with navy slacks and flats, but hey, I would still do me. Today was way too eventful for a first day back, but hey, I successfully Call-of-Dutied my way to my office today! Wish you could have seen me! I army crawled, ninja jumped, threw a few flying star thingies, it was epic. Well, goodnight....
Tomorrow I have to go back to the land of the insane.
<3 Hope

My Friends

I have three friends, and Ray is the stud muffin out of the group. He is six-foot-six, toned, smart, and African American. Sean is a weirdo who has tons of Bang friends and plays video games all day, and then there is Jen, the loudmouthed, five-foot-seven brunette bombshell who has the mouth of a sailor. Let's meet them all so you guys can feel my pain.

JEN

We first met in a bar; I was drunk and sad, and she was drunk and, well…let's just say outgoing. Here's what happened.

As we all know, Hanky and I had broken up and now was the time for me to recuperate. Well I did, but not in pretty way…more like in public. I went to the bar with me, myself, and I. I began to drink margaritas and took a few shots of Mr. José. Soon I was face deep in tears on the bar counter. On the other side of the bar, there she was, all five feet, seven inches, brunette, loudmouthed-like-a-sailor-with-boobs-out Jen. She was screaming, "Wahoo and eff guys! I'm hot and ya'll suck!" Apparently she'd gotten dumped and was handling it in a different manner. She began to table dance like she was in the movie *Coyote Ugly*, ringing the bar

19

bell and buying everyone drinks. Her motions were making me sick, so I got up and ran to the bathroom. I began to throw up in the single-stall ladies' room. Soon Jen was right behind me, wanting to hurl too. She was so hammered she didn't even see me bent over the toilet. So if you can't guess what happened next, I'll tell you: This bitch threw up on my head.

Soon the little bit of throw-up in my hair wasn't so important. Jen was a hottie, so for her to get dumped made me feel 10 times better. We shared stories and tears about our exes in the bathroom, and she helped me clean my hair in the sink. Shortly after that, a friendship developed into a sisterhood. Jen and I were inseparable while dealing with our breakups. She got fat and ate Chunky Monkey ice cream with me and worked it off with me months later. We cried and watched *Dirty Dancing* and threw darts at Hanky's picture, which we'd hung on the wall. Jen even let me room with her while I emptied Hanky's and my apartment. Talk about a real soul sister. Jen even went as far as copying a scene from Ashton Kutcher and Cameron Diaz's movie *What Happens in Vegas*. She pulled a Tipper and went to Hanky's mom's house, rang the doorbell, and waited for him to answer the door. She was kneeling, and as soon as Hanky answered, she cranked back and junk-punched him. He cried and said, "WHYY!?" and she said, "YOU KNOW WHY!" Ahh, classic Tipper moment. Now I know you're wondering about Jen and why such a doll like her got dumped. Well, here is her story.

Jen's Break Up

Jen met a guy named James at the gym she worked at. Since she is a personal trainer, she saw tons of hotties every day of the week. James was a regular; he usually just did cardio and minimal lifting. James was six-foot-four, Caucasian with a naturally tinted complexion, nice, well-educated, and ridiculously handsome. This guy was photoshopped. It's weird that he hardly touched weights because he had the body of a *300* character. Anyway, he peeped her out as she was helping a group of high school kids get in shape for track season. He first pretended that he wanted to build more muscle, but really he just wanted to get her number and take her out.

Jen usually wasn't this smitten with guys, but James seemed like the perfect guy for her. Soon they began taking their gym relationship out in public. They would watch movies, go to dinners, and hang with each other's families. They went four months strong with no sex; instead they had great conversation and exceptional company. But Jen was a sex fiend, and she had to at least test drive the car before making a full-on commitment. One night James spent the night over at Jen's house. They both fell asleep while watching the cute romantic comedy *Jumping the Broom*. She woke up before him and decided she would try to seduce him that night.

She slipped away from laying on his chest and tiptoed into the bathroom. She jumped into the shower, got all dolled up, and slipped into a sexy corset. She then hopped on him like he was a horse, slowly making her way to his ear.

"Hey, handsome, wake up."

James smiled and opened his eyes a little bit.. "Hey, Jen, what ya doing? Oh, look at you! You look hot!"

"It's for you." She slowly started to take off his shirt and tried to kiss his chest. He jumped up and said, "I'm waiting for the right one, Jen, let's not rush things. I have to go and meet some friends at a bar tonight. I'm sorry, but I really have to go. I'll call you later."

James split as fast as he could. Jen was very confused and hurt. Since she was up and sexy, she figured she might as well hit the bars tonight too. She picked up her phone and tried to call all her girls to come party hardy, but for some reason they were all booed up. Jen decided to go out solo anyways. She walked into Heat, one of the hottest bars in Arizona, and immediately headed towards the bar.

She ordered her usual lemon drop, along with a

margarita and an extra shot of Patron Silver. She loved the music and made her way to the dance floor. As she spun around she saw James in between the legs of someone else. Soon she saw a nicely manicured hand grip his back and pull him close. She zoomed in and watched patiently as her blood began to boil.

She made her way slowly towards him, creeping up ninja style. As she went to tap his shoulder, the person in the chair stood up to whisper something dirty into James's ear. Who she saw pretty much made her throw up. James was gay. Turned out he wasn't just waiting for the right one, he was waiting for this guy, apparently.

James's lover took his hand and tried to direct him to the dance floor, where they ran into a very drunk Jen on the bar flipping him off and taking body shots. James mouthed the words *I'm sorry*. In retaliation, Jen got up and yelled, "F GUYS, THEY SUCK.... LITTERALLY!"

RAY

He loves the ladies and they love him too. How did we meet? Well, he's my brother-in-law's brother. He is the EXACT opposite of his brother; not only is Ray opened-minded, but he is not attracted to white chicks at all. Why? Well, because he says we are psycho crazy. Instead, in order to be with Ray, you have to be Spanish or black. That's called for some interesting mixes when he's brought girls around our circle.

Ray is a true man's man; he loves the gym, sports, and food. He opens doors for the ladies and becomes their knight in shining armor. So why is this lovely piece of meat alone? Well, if you can't tell by my coworkers and Jen, he's not all there, like the rest of us.

Ray is a love guru and, surprisingly, knows how to get people together and keep it that way. He's a matchmaker for hookmeup.com, which is pretty much a knockoff of Match and eHarmony but instead, when you go to the website, you see his sexy face and abs. There's also a little bubble that reads, *You can get a guy with abs like mine. Click for your trial offer.* Yeah, I know, a little rough around the edges, but it brings people in somehow.

Every time Ray meets a girl, he brings her around our circle and for some reason they always run away. Now it's not because of my shyness or Jen's blunt assholeness or even Sean's strange *World of Warcraft* email invites. It's because of Ray. All the height, sexiness, and brains can't hide the fact that he is an emotional, clingy baby. That's right, Ray will blow up your phone, send ridiculous amounts of flowers to your job and house, and even propose three months in because he's completely smitten. Ray is a muscled teddy bear who loves being in love and the thought of it, hence hookmeup.com.

Soon on the couch there were three of us eating Chunky Monkey during this sorrowful time. Me, Jen, and yup, Mr. "Teary Eyes" Ray. Can you say friendship?

SEAN

Now let's discuss Sean. He's the awkward friend who stays on the computer or some kind of device 24/7. Sean is average height, around five-foot-ten, and is Indian—like the dot, not the feathers.

Sean and I met after I trashed my computer and had to take it to NerdCrew. Not only did those jerks ruin my computer, they made it worse. So instead I looked up local computer fixer uppers. There it was in Google: Arizona Computer Fixer Upper Kings. Yes that's the name of his shop. I took my laptop in and there he was. Sean. He spun around in his leather chair, glasses on along with a headset, holding a slushie from Mr. King's Grocery. He stared at me until I spoke. Clearly this guy didn't like starting conversation.

"So, I need help with my computer."

"Obviously."

"Alright, umm, can you help?"

"Yes, I am the KING! Put it there, let me see." I placed my laptop on the counter. "Whoa! How old is this baby?"

"Umm, she's a few years young."

"Yeah, and so is the pope. This baby is what, from the early nineties has to be."

"Well try late eighties."

"OH my! BOYS! Come here, we have found the Battlestar Galactica of laptops." Soon there were about five to seven nerds behind the biggest one, oohing and ahhing. It got on my nerves!

"Okay, okay! I know I am a little outdated…"

"A LITTLE?" they said in unison.

"Yeah, try outdated by two decades plus! It's twenty thirteen, lady! Okay, I can try to work with her but it will take a couple weeks."

"Wow, really? That long?"

"Yes, that long. This baby needs to be handled with care and she needs to be taken apart nice and slow."

"Okay, well I'll see you in a week."

He waved me away as he made love to my computer in his mind. Yes, I have a laptop from the '80s! It still works (well did) and it's very reliable. A week went by so I decided to give the shop a call and see where they were at exactly.

"Arizona Computer Fixer Upper Kings."

"Hi, this is Hope. I gave you guys my laptop a while ago and was wondering about the status?"

"Oh yeah. Ms. Hope, aka Director of the Battlestar Galactica."

"No, no. Just Hope."

"Alright, Athena, one sec, let me get Sean."

"Who's Athena?"

"You."

"No, I'm Hope."

"Yeah, and you're Athena. She's a lieutenant for the Battlestar Galactica. One second!" Oh my… what did I get myself into. "Hey, Sean, I have Athena on the phone calling about her mother ship!"

"Athena. S'up?"

"It's Hope, and what's up with the computer?"

"Oh yeah, it died."

"WHAT!?"

"Athena, chill. That baby is old, get a new one."

"No, I love that one."

"Yeah, and so did Jesus when he brought it with him after he was resurrected. I put all the files on a thumb drive, and you can upload them to your new computer."

"What computer should I get?"

27

And that question alone sparked a conversation that lasted over two hours on the phone. Since I was tying up his phone line we decided to meet at Best Buy. There we roamed side by side, me getting schooled on computers and other updated devices.

"So, thanks for coming with me, Sean."

"You're welcome, Athena. So you're pretty cool, let's be Bang friends."

"Um, I don't have a Bang."

He spit out his slushie and stared at me for a couple seconds.

"WHAT! Who doesn't have Bang? I have thousands of friends. Not to toot my own horn, but TOOT, TOOT! I kick ass, and you're an ass for not having one."

"OUCH! Whoa! What's the big deal?"

"Well, I guess if you have to ask then you have no business having one. I guess we can be real friends. Take my digits, and if we get drunk one night don't take advantage of me."

The next day I was having Jen and Ray over for some drinks and talk time before we decided to watch movies. This time I invited Sean. Before he came I figured I would tell the two that I added someone new to the group.

"So guys..."

"What up!" said Jen.

"Well, there is someone coming over."

"Oooh, does this someone have a penis?" asked Ray.

"Umm, yes."

"Name?" asked Jen.

"Sean."

"Date of birth, height, credit score—"

"WHOA, RAY! He is NOT a date! Not by any means.... Ewwww."

"Then why is he coming over?" asked Jen.

"Because he is a really cool guy and I figured that he could join the circle."

"BUT I'M THE GUY! That's how this works, a hot guy with two—" He glanced at me. "—well sort of two hotties."

"Thanks, Ray." I said.

"Well, muscle bags has a point, the guy thing is HIS thing."

"But I know he will fit in nicely, just give him a chance."

"Alright, but if he's a weirdo he has to go," said Ray.

Soon enough, after another glass of wine, the doorbell rang. Jen and Ray looked at each other and prayed that this wasn't a random stray that I brought home again. I ran to answer it with a humungous smile on my face.

"SEAN!"

"S'up, Athena," Sean said as he came into my house sipping a big slushie.

"Okay, so the gang is in here—"

"Gang? Is this an initiation? Are you trying to tie me up and touch my goodies?"

"Umm, no. Follow me this way." We walked into the kitchen, talking under our breath to each other along the way.

"Hey, guys…" Jen and Ray turned around.

"Oooh, hey, Hope, she can touch my goodies anytime."

"Dream on, freak face," said Jen.

"Hey, calm it down, Barbie Sailor Mouth," shot back Sean.

"HA! I like him!" said Ray.

"What's so funny, muscle butt?" said Sean.

"HA! NO! I like him!" said Jen. "You're in."

"In what?" Sean asked.

"The gang. You're cool, you have a sharp tongue. That's very much a necessity when hanging with Jen," said Ray.

"Well, I can be her necessity," said Sean as he pursed his lips.

"Ugh, whatever, Gandhi."

Ahh, I knew it! Good one, Hope. Another great addition to the clan. In a matter of minutes we became best friends. There we were during the breakups, Jen and Ray on the couch with me, eating ice cream, and Sean behind the couch slurping that damn slushie. After the movie we walked into the kitchen. We struck up a conversation about how we hate guys and girls. Ray said he'd deleted his latest love on his Bang site, and Jen threw in a comment on how it's not official until it's Bang official. Then Sean chimed in and mentioned to the group, "Hope doesn't have a Bang." Soon all eyes were on me and the questions came, followed by demanding statements.

"So, you're gay." said Jen.

"That's what I said!" blurted Sean.

"You need Bang. No wonder why you're single!" said Ray.

So began my journey towards being updated on slaps (the equivalent of Facebook poking), messages, and a hot display pic. What had I gotten myself into?

* * *

Dear Diary (and people reading this and snooping around),

This is how we all became friends and how I got to where I am and why I hate and I mean HATE social networking. I guess it's time to let the story unfold. Don't judge me.

< 3 Have No More Control Hop

Just Me and Bang

Alright, so there we were, me and the computer, the computer-o and I. I typed in bang.com and pulled up a horrific-looking website. It was outlined in yellow, the link buttons were orange and turned to pink once you clicked on them, and it had the face of some random guy right along the left side. His face took up the entire left side with a very awkward smile. He was pasty white with brown eyes and red hair (weird, right?). It took me about 10 minutes to find the *Create an account* button, mainly because I was stalling.

So I sucked it up and went ahead and made the account. They asked so many questions on there! Like what's your email and phone number, pictures, bio, and hobbies. My gosh, is nothing private anymore? No wonder why all these weird people are being hacked up on these sites; you can put your ENTIRE life onto one page.

I scrolled through the question to see which ones I wanted to answer.

Bio: Well, I am awesome and I like to read

Status: Widow

Hobbies: *Loving life*

Everything else I left blank. Why did I put *Widow* for status? Well, it felt like it ever since Hanky and I split, I'd been feeling kinda dead. Now it was time to put up a picture. I sorted through all my pics on my laptop and couldn't find one that really screamed *Hope*, so I picked the next best thing: I Googled something that I absolutely love! Now my profile was complete. It was basic and the pic was adorable. Man, do I love kittens, especially ones with sweaters.

Sitting at my computer I realized the amount of time it took to make the profile, upload pictures, add friends, and so forth. People are on this thing all day! On iPhones, iPods', and Nooks, and they all download the apps—the gossipy, brain-sucking, time-wasting apps—for what? To stay tuned in with the world and what people are doing? See, when I was growing up, we had one number and a plug-in for internet and had to wait our turn. Now, since everything is so accessible, I wonder what privacy is left.

I decided to fool around on Bang for awhile and look up people that I knew. I first typed in my boss's name, and sure enough, she popped right up. The heifer had over two thousand people! Then, when I looked through her pictures, I realized why: being half-naked and sexy, plus a blond, would put icing on anyone's cake. I was disgusted by the comments men were leaving, like *Damn sexy I want to be that drink between your legs* to *Umm umm umm wanna bang?* And it got worse. Where's the chivalry?

I decided to look up my friends and check them out. Jen had her profile on private so I couldn't see much but her name and profile pic. Sean had his set on a random setting to where I could look at things, but only things he allowed, which mainly consisted of *Star Wars* costumes and *Galactica* posters that had his face photoshopped in. Now as for Ray, his was as open as Kelly's profile, mainly because he has a business that helps you find love. So when people Google him he allows his Bang account to pop up. Ray's profile picture had his arms folded and eyebrow raised, kind of a cheesy smile, and a tight-ass black tee shirt. His profile contained quotes from Gandhi and other inspirational messages, and his pictures showcased love matches and one random picture of him wearing all white and walking on rocks.

So, I'm not going to lie, these guys made my profile seem like a piece of cat dung. Back to the drawing board I went. I stared at my profile again and looked at things I could change and add. Problem was, I'm a very private person! So adding religious beliefs, political views, and real pictures scared the crap out of me. After my 10-minute hyperventilation session, I snapped back into reality and kept my profile the way it was. If people wanted to know me, they would ask, right?

I looked at the clock and noticed I'd wasted almost three hours on this damn website, and that was only in trying to create a profile and looking at four people. Man, I couldn't imagine what it would be like when I got this thing up and running. No wonder people get hooked; it's like crack but for the brain.

Taking a break from the world I so passionately hated, I jumped in the shower and sang to my fans; the shampoo and conditioner had been without a concert for a week now. NOT saying I hadn't showered or anything; I just hadn't serenaded them with my fabulous voice. After a 45-minute concert I exited the shower and began to sing into my blow dryer. Staring at myself in the mirror I realized I'm one sexy beast, and for someone to not love me and want me, well, they are stupid.

Leaving my concert headquarters I went into the kitchen, towel-wrapped and hair semi-dry, and grabbed my friend Chunky Monkey. Even though I worked it off I can still have a scoop or two—or a pint—every now and again.

As I was beginning to enjoy my day off, my phone was being blown up by my lovely friends asking about this damn Bang account. "Did you create one?" "Why haven't you added us?" "What picture did you use?" "Are you half-naked?" Wait, what? Damn it, Sean! Anyways, I ignored them all continued, eating my Chunky Monkey, and relaxed the rest of the day.

* * *

Dear Diary,

So I spent three hours on Bang and didn't realize it. I wasn't doing anything productive on it, either! This is already starting to scare me
<3 The Superstitious Hope

Banging at Work

I can't lie: Waking up and going to work the next day was a little weird. I mean, I caved and made a Bang account. Since Kelly was out of the office for lipo— Oops! I mean "a stomachache," I had time to do whatever the hell I wanted.

So I didn't waste my entire day. I made a few boring calls to companies, trying to get them to buy our awesome pens. I also sat in the bathroom and tried to find a few people who were willing to play battle shits, and when that didn't work I used the men's room. Then, after all of that, I decided to spin in my chair until I got dizzy enough to take a nap (trust me, that is not recommended).

After two hours of no sales, multiple potty breaks, and a great nap time, I got a phone call. Reluctant to answer it, I let the call go to voicemail. Soon enough, whoever it was called back three times in a row! So I figured I might as well...

"Sharps, this is Hope."

"Athena, s'up."

"Sean?"

"Yeah, I have muscle bags and sailor mouth here, too."

"Hey!" said Ray.

" Die off, geek squad." We all know who that was.

"Hey, guys, what's going on?"

"We all played hooky today," said Sean.

"Really?"

"Yes, bizatch," said Jen.

"So come on! Let's go!" said Ray.

"What do you mean, 'let's go'?"

"We're on the other side of the glass. Look up," said Sean.

I reluctantly lifted my head and saw them, my three stooges, Moe, Larry, and Curly, waving like they hadn't seen me in forever. They walked to my desk in a hurry shortly, all of them hovering over my personal space.

"So what are we doing if I ditch?"

"Bang! And it's Friday, so we have a head start on the weekend! So come on, Athena!" said Sean.

"For your information, I made a Bang."

"Really? Let's see it then, cupcake," said Ray.

I was more than happy to pull up my creation. I logged onto my account and showed them my profile. They all looked at each other and laughed.

"Kitten," Ray said.

"I love kittens."

"You're allergic," stated Jen.

"Wait a minute, Athena has some messages!"

Now I was as surprised as they were. Me, Hope, with the display picture as a kitten, had messages? Ray jumped through the middle of Jen and Sean, grabbed the mouse, and started to sort through my messages.

"Okay, look, this guy named Jordan. He seems okay, nice face and build, good smile, and—"

"Whoa, muscles, so are you looking at him for Hope or for you?"

"Hope! Duh, Sean!"

"Well you could've fooled us," spat Jen.

"Anyway! Jordan says, 'Hey, sexy face, I love your coat.'" They all looked at each other and started laughing. Jen turned red, Sean couldn't breathe, and Ray looked slightly disturbed.

"Oh let's read some more!" said Sean as he grabbed the mouse and clicked on message number two. "Okay so this dork named Brian said, 'Hey Hope, I always have hope in my life, how about you get some Brian in yours?'"

"HA! This is CLASSIC!" said Jen.

"Alright, enough laughing at my expense." I tried to take the conversation back and get everyone to focus and not just focus on the freaks that roam social networking sites.

"Not so fast, Athena, let's check out your profile." Sean then scrolled down my profile. He shook his head at the things he read.

"So you're a widow?" Sean asked.

"Well, I might as well be."

"And who did you add?" asked Ray.

"Well, you guys, of course!"

"Who else, lame tard?" asked Jen.

"Well, no one. I tried but I got denied."

"Who wants to add a widowed kitten? That's right, NO ONE!" yelled Sean.

"Okay, okay, I see I need major help with this."

"Duh, biznatch! And that's why we are here!"

"Why are you here?"

"To revamp you," said Ray.

"Umm guys..."

"Yeah, make you sexy" said Sean.

"Push them boobies up, stick that booty out, and get a mizan!" said Jen, of course.

"WAIT A MINUTE! Why am I the one having to get a man?"

"Because your eggs are frying! You're like forty—" said Sean.

"Thirty-two."

"Yeah, whatever, and your clock is ticking," Sean said.

"I am a guru at love matching," stated Ray.

"Except for yourself, muscle brain," blurted Sean.

"Sean, be nice, he's sensitive," said Jen as she made a kissy face and pinched Ray's cheeks.

Great, I was getting a Bang profile makeover from a sailor, a muscle head and a nerd. The new me should be interesting. We didn't leave my office like we had planned; instead I had to sit there and let the three stooges work on my profile—changing pictures, adding pictures, creating an About Me and plugging in my political beliefs. I wasn't allowed to see this new profile until the next day, so this whole day I was banned from a computer and had to agree to let things stay as they made it.

FINALLY! After about 45 minutes they were done and we were able to leave work. Packing into my small car we headed to the mall to grab some Yogo.

"So, Athena, cats in sweaters. Is that like a fetish or something?"

"Sean.... No, I just love them, like I said before."

"Yes, she loves things she can't touch because she's deathly allergic," chimed in Jen.

"I'm just asking because I don't want you to be alone

forever. You're already headed in that direction. So adding cats to a site that can open your whole entire world seems pretty dumb."

Everyone else agreed. They didn't say so, but since no one spoke up and just looked at me while they ate their Yogo, it was clear enough.

"Yeah, guys, so I'm beat, I'm gonna head home. Want me to drop y'all off?" I said.

"No, it's cool, we can call someone," said Ray.

So there I was, walking out of the mall trying not to cry. Did my life seem so sad and pathetic that it seemed I may end up alone? Was it really that bad? So what, I'm in my thirties, no kids, no boyfriend, no sex, and no love interest. Instead I have a crappy car, a dead-end job, and friends.

I hated long car rides and that day was the worst. For some reason my radio wouldn't work, which left just me and my thoughts. Great.

What usually takes about 30 minutes to get from the main mall to *mi casa* took over an hour. Not only did I leave during rush hour, for one, but my car stopped and stalled four times (and my car is an automatic). The radiator was smoking because I ran out of fluids. I had to putt-putt my car to the gas station, and no one would let me over. All while birds were attacking my windshield. So I was blinded by shit and had no radio and a smoking car that didn't want to run in the middle of a hot-ass day in Tucson, Arizona.

Throwing myself onto my couch, I laid there—no movement, no motions to pick up the ringing phone or turn on the television. I just needed some time and space. Ever have one of those days? I wanted to scream my head off but had no energy. I also wanted a drink but didn't want to get up.

Look at me, I was making this a pity party! And I hate pity parties! Yeah, the day sucked, and yes, my friends said some harsh things, but in reality I knew they were true. I just didn't want to face it. Sucks how much your life is examined once you put it all on paper, huh?

I got off the couch and popped in a movie. Then I headed into the kitchen and heated up some burnt leftovers that Jen had made; it was supposed to be spaghetti, but it looked like rock balls with tomato paste and hard shoe laces.

After a nice quiet dinner and a movie, I settled my little sourpuss butt into the tub, turned on some soft music, and began to ease my mind. In the tub I slowly lifted my legs, looking at the soap, watching it slowly bead down into the water. I played with my hair as it crinkled up and stared at my fingers and toes as they began to look like my grandpa's. Even in a room with complete serenity, I still found my mind racing.

It took about 10 minutes until I was able to calm my thoughts. I hadn't realized it, but my phone was blowing up! I didn't want to speak to anyone so I figured I could answer the texts. They were all from Jen, and when I say "all," I mean all 20 text messages. She likes to do this thing when she texts my whole name letter by letter then sends it. Ugh, I hate it, but oh well. Here's what it went like:

Jen: Hey BITCH! I'm getting my dancing on tonight wanna come?

Me: HOPE is my name, and where are you?

Jen: SO I found this guy and….

Me: Oh man, so I'll be home at 6….. AM!

Drunk texts from Jen are always the best. With that being said, I could expect my happy quiet time to be disturbed as she stumbled in. In the midst of these messages, I received one from my sister:

"Hey sis, still on for spa day tomorrow?"

Shit! I had totally spaced it! But of course this was our family weekend! We try to do one at least one a month now. A whole weekend dedicated to family, with Sunday being the family dinner, aka wrap up.

* * *

Dear Diary,

Words hurt, but hide your emotions and cover up your feelings and reality hurts even more. I shouldn't be so sour towards my friends. They were right. Am I that afraid of change? I won't always be alone, will I? When is a good time for a life makeover? So many questions to a book that can't give me the answers. At least I have family day starting tomorrow, so that will lift me up a little. Right?
<3 The Confused, Hurt, Smacked-in-the–Face-with -Reality Hope

Family Time

I woke up at eight and was surprised that I hadn't been awoken by Jen and her man date. Now, do I get nervous when she brings home random men? Of course I do because I don't want to end up on Investigation Discovery or CNN. I trust Jen, but not her men, which is why I have a nice pistol under my pillow. I'm a smart cookie.

Heading into the bathroom I smelled vomit, KY Jelly, latex, and tequila. I peeked into Jen's room and saw a man's foot sticking off out her bed and blond hair on the other side. Well at least they would be sleep until I left. I went into my concert stadium (aka the bathroom) and slowly closed the door. When I turned on the light I saw a random redhead in our bathtub. Not being too sure of what I was seeing, I turned off and on the lights repeatedly, and to my surprise, there she was, a random redhead, K.O. in our tub, snoring and half-naked.

So I sat there, brushed my teeth, and poked her with my loofa. I started to floss my teeth and kept poking the random hooker in my bathroom, and she still didn't wake up. I even started playing my music, singing along, and styled my hair while poking the hooker, and she was still snoring. I was able to drop a deuce and make breakfast without anyone waking up! So as I was about to leave to get my sis, I decided to pour water on Jen and her man friend.

"WHOA! Bitch! WHAT'S UP?! You should've came out with us last night, it was epic!" said Jen.

"Yeah, I see. You have a hooker in the tub."

"Megan?" asked random guy.

"I don't know. Redhead?"

"Yeah, Megan. She was fun," said random guy.

"Jen?"

"Oh, this is Mark."

"Alex."

"Oh, my bad. This is Alex, Alex this is Hope."

"S'up, Hope! You didn't want to join the sexy party?"

"No, it's not her thing. Hope, is she okay in there?"

"Yeah, I think so. She didn't move when I was poking her, but she's snoring."

"Yeah, Megan likes to be poked."

"Shut up, Stan!" said Jen.

"It's Alex," he and I said in unison.

"Whatever! So where you headed?"

"It's family weekend."

"Oh yeah, tell them I say hi!"

Closing the door behind me was the best thing I could've ever done to save my breakfast and keep it down. Leaving my house I felt as if it was going to be a great day.

"Lindsey!" I said as I saw my sister in the parking lot of the nail salon.

"Hey, you! What's goin' on? Ready to get sexy?"

"Of course!"

Don't worry; during family dinner you will get the whole rundown on my sister and her evilness.

We sat in the pedicure chairs and started to talk about work and the nail colors we were going to get done when she asked this: "So, Hope, what's wrong? I can sense it a mile away."

I took a deep breath and told her about Bang and

creating one and also what my friends had said about me and being old and whatnot. She sat and listened to me vent for half of the pedicure time. When I stopped talking to calm down because I was getting a headache, my sister added in, "Well, Hope, I love you, but you know they are right in a way. You have this bubble, this guard up, and you need to just release that sometimes. Let go and let loose. I know I am not good at letting loose, but I'm also married with kids and you aren't, so live."

Hearing what she had to say after the depth of our conversation drove me crazy. Was no one going to be on my side with this? After our pedicures we got a manicure and continued to talk about life.

After the nail salon we went to the mall, saw a movie, and also ate. Today was the perfect sister day without my demonic nieces and nephews around. Before we knew it, it was six p.m. and we were headed home.

"So are you going to church in the morning? "

"Yeah, I'll see you guys there! What time is it at again?"

"HOPE!"

"I'm just joking! Geez!! Haha, I'll be there."

When I walked into the house, it was quiet, no Jen in site. I found a note on the remote saying:

Out with Alex and I'll see you after your family time tomorrow. Hugs and kisses <3 Jen. By the way if I text 911 means come save me because dude is cray cray!

Another night alone!? Oh my, what did I do to deserve such a relaxing weekend? I popped open that bottle of wine, threw in another movie, and sat in my Snuggie and relaxed the entire night.

I woke up feeling refreshed and happy. Jen was in her room; she must have tiptoed in. I got ready for church and started to make my way there.

At first my Sunday started off pretty normal. I tried to hear the gospel of God. Yes, I said *tried*; there was a kid poking at the back of my neck and using my shoulder as his ramp for his toy car. The lesson obviously had to be pretty good because everyone was shouting and praising while I was trying not to beat this kid into another dimension. His mother was no help at all; she just smiled and said, "Kids will be kids." I smiled back, thinking, *And my hand has no self-control either.*

After a long and grueling service, I jumped in my car thinking about my mom's food. Now, she isn't a good cook by any means! My mom, however, is a great baker; I already knew the dessert would make up for the evening meal. This night it was meatloaf. Sounds basic, right? Well, last time my mom added jelly beans and cream cheese because it gave the meatloaf a certain pizzazz! Meanwhile, it didn't agree with my stomach, and I became well-acquainted with my porcelain, powder-pink toilet. This night's side dishes included macaroni and cheese, lima beans, and squash. The squash is usually raw and the lima beans are typically still hard. Oh, yummy! I was hoping that dinner would be canceled; I really didn't want to go.

I tried to start my car and nothing happened. No lights turned on, no dinging noise, no engine turned over. Seriously, Lord? The one time I joke about not wanting to go somewhere you actually make it so I don't get there? Where was this when I needed your eyes with Hanky? Ugh! I hated everything at that point.

I called my parents' house, telling them I wasn't going to make it to family night. My dad all of a sudden put his hero hat on and decided he was going to come and get me. I rolled my eyes and said okay, then I waited patiently for him to come.

"Hey, sweetie!"

"Hey, pops! "

"Looks like you have a little oops here! It's okay, hop on in." I got into Dad's car, buckled my seatbelt, and noticed him staring weirdly into my face.

"So, Dad, what's up?"

"Well, Hope, your family is worried about you. Now, I'm giving you warning because when we get to the house, things might be weird."

"Weirder than you staring into my face?"

"Yes, well, Mom thinks you're batting for the other team an—"

"What?"

"—and Linds thinks you might be on the road to kill yourself—"

"HUH!? What the hell!"

"—and Uncle Mike wants to move in with you so he can monitor you so you don't kill yourself off and—"

"DAD! I'm not a lesbo, I don't want to die, and Uncle Mike just wants to have sex with Jen."

"Yes I know all that's true except—"

"Except what?!"

"Well your recent hairdo speaks wonders. Hahaha, I'm just kidding, hun. I know you! Just giving you a warning!"

Great, I couldn't wait for dinner now. Soon we rolled up to my parents' house and I sat in the car for a little while, wishing and hoping that I didn't have to go in.

Here's a little rundown of my random and dysfunctional family.

Lindsey and Ryan

Alrighty. So Lindsey—you got a little taste of her while I was getting my nails done—of course is my sister, and Ryan is Ray's brother, aka my brother-in-law. Together they have two kids, but Ryan brought two into their marriage, bringing the Brady Bunch clan to four kids. Ryan is shorter than Ray, about five-foot-nine, stocky, and kind-hearted. My sister, on the other hand, is a demanding, Satan wannabe. She's blond with green eyes and perky boobs. She kept her shape after having two kids, but her attitude has gotten really bad. I think it's because she stays at home all the time and finds herself hating her married life. She smiles in front of everyone, but with me she unleashes. She told me it's not Ryan himself, it's the fact that she settled at a young age because she thought she was in love then. Ryan is so passive it turns my sister off sometimes. Did you know the last time those two got freaky was when my five-year-old niece was conceived?! Talk about drought!

Uncle Michael
Now here is my uncle Michael, or Big Mike. He is stuck in the '80s and is a playboy. He gets the ladies and

never sleeps alone. Imagine Pierce Brosnan as double-oh seven with a grey streak in the front of his hair and a golden tan. My uncle used to be an actor (an extra) in many movies. He's kept his swagger for years and hasn't changed his lingo at all

Mom & Pops

Now I told you a little about my mom, aka Hellen. She loves to be in the kitchen, even though it should only be for baking. She's the type that decorates the house on Halloween and Christmas. Mom loves unicorns and anything that has to do with rainbows, so you can only imagine what our house looked like. One time my friends came over when I was like eight years old. Nancy touched my mom's unicorn, and I swear Mom flipped so much shit she was shitting glitter! Talk about panic attack meets hyperventilation. My dad, aka Bill, on the other hand, is a real man's man. Loves sports, dirt, cars, and anything that bleeds. He's a regular Bob the Builder but doesn't exactly know how to make anything work. One time when Mom was on vacation he tried to replace a light socket cover and he electrocuted himself. That was an interesting talk with police as to why his 10-year-old daughter was driving him to the ER.

Back to Dinner

Alright, so where did I leave off…. That's right! We pulled up to my parents' house. My badass nephews and niece were running around screaming, my mom was singing and dancing in the kitchen, and well, my brother-in-law was being yelled at by my sister; the perfect normal Sunday was finally here. Why on earth would I want to miss this?

I got out of the car and immediately got love from my nephews but not my niece; she's a freakin' weirdo. Her name is Melissa but everyone calls her Hissy. Why do we call her that? Well the little tard brain hisses all the damn time. She's friggin' six and won't speak but she'll hiss the hell out of a conversation. So I hugged my manly men of nephews: Trey, who tries to shave; Michael, who wears his dad's cologne; and Albert, who likes dirt. As for Melissa, well she loves pigtails, polka dots, and hissing. Oh yeah, and the movie *The Omen*; nice, right?

I gathered them up and we headed inside to sit at the table of love…or of awkwardness mixed with confrontation. Everything seemed normal and cool until after grace was said, and then the table turned into a World War III battlefield.

"Hand me the beans," demanded my lovely sister,

Lindsey. No one answered her when it was clear she was talking to Ryan. "Hey, I said pass the beans!"

"I know what you said, but that's not how you ask." Rage soon filled her pale face and I began to laugh a little. Ryan never puts my sister in check; he's a nerdy man who obeys orders. It's pretty disgusting to me. He went on to say, "You say 'Please,' or 'Can you pass the beans.' You don't demand things. That's why Melissa is as bad as she is, she gets it from her mother!"

"Oh, the hell with you! I'll get the beans myself since I do everything myself anyway."

"Sounds good to me!"

"Ugh, I don't know why you gave us your blessing, Dad! He's a complete moron!"

"And it goes both ways," said Dad. HA! How I love him.

"Daddy!" said Lindsey. "You're supposed to be on my side!"

"I don't have sides, I have eyes. And the way you treat him is wrong."

"But—"

"'But' my ass. You're grown and so is he. It's not my business, but son, let me tell you something. STOP BEING SUCH A PUSSWAGON!!" Yes, that's right, my dad didn't call Ryan a jackwagon, instead he called him a pusswagon! He makes up awesome words all the time. Makes me giggle.

"Well, let's lighten the mood," said Mother dearest as she changed the subject to me. "So, my dear Hope, what did you want to discuss?" I was blindsided because I wanted to have this ridiculous convo in private.

"Oh, nothing, Mom. I'll tell you later."

"Oh, what, you're too perfect to talk in front of everyone?" snapped Lindsey.

"Um, no, Cruela, it's none of your business, just between me and Mom."

"Well, honey, I'm sure we all can help."

"Yeah, Hope, we all can help," said Ryan. I looked at my jellybean meatloaf, swallowed my tongue and pride, and began to speak.

"Well the asses want me to join Bang and begin dating again."

"Okay, now that wasn't hard, pumpkin face!" said Daddy.

"What's the big deal?" asked Ryan.

"Well I don't want to!"

"Why?" asked my nephew Trey. "Bang is a great way to make friends and meet potential men, and Auntie, I want to see you happy."

"And get LAID!" said Michael, who, not to mention, was around 10 and had found his new love for internet porn. Ryan and my dad busted out laughing while my mom and Lindsey looked appalled. I thought it was funny but didn't want to laugh because I was sitting way too close to my mom.

So after that random outburst, I proceeded to plead my case about how lame Bang was and how it wouldn't help me at all. Then my smartass brother-in-law walked us over to the computer and showed me what Bang can do. We logged on to my account, and let's just say I hated what I saw, and trust me, it was all Jen's, Sean's and Ray's doing.

"Alright, Hope! Let's see what your— Oh, my 'LANTA!" We all looked at my display pic in shock. My sister laughed and said my boobs were fake, my dad squinted and said it looked like a *Playboy* model reject, and my mom cried. Apparently my picture was changed to one of this horrendous-looking female. Her boobs were ginormous, her lips were definitely injected with something, and her waist was nonexistent, but hey, at least the hair color was right, despite the clown makeup job. Photoshop isn't supposed to be used by people who are functional idiots!

"Dang, Auntie, you have a lot of slaps!" said Albert.

"What are slaps?" asked Trey.

"It's when a man takes his peni—"

"MICHAEL!" we all said in unison. This kid needed a muzzle and spyware protection. Lindsey rolled her eyes at her son while his dad gave him a low five.

"Well, Hope, you seem to be quite the catch on Bang, you've been slapped and have about ten friend requests waiting for ya. Now let's look at your About Me info."

"Hey look, big boobs has some messages! " said Lindsey.

"Oh! Let's read them! Maybe they want to be her friend," Mom said.

"With that picture, I'm sure they will be more than friends, honey," said Dad.

"What's that mean?"

"Nothing, honey, let's check out her messages."

Putting my head down, I could only imagine the messages I would've gotten since the profile makeover. I mean, if weirdoes were messaging me because I had a cat picture up, I was pretty sure they would have a lot to say after seeing this *Playboy* picture.

"Okay!" said Lindsey. "Trent said, 'Your boobs bring out your hair.' Way to pick 'em, Hope." As she scrolled down the messages she sorted through guys saying things like, *Your face is hot*, or *I wanna be your shirt*, or, my favorite of the day, *Is there any chance I can be IN some Hope?* Yeah, guys are awesome!

"Hey, Hope, looks like you have a stalker on your hands. Trent messaged you about three more times within thirty minutes of each other. He wants to know why you guys aren't Bang friends yet and why you haven't slapped him back."

"Oh, honey, you need to change your display picture, it's sending the wrong impression," said Mom.

"And like putting a real one of her up will be sending a better one?" said Lindsey.

"Lindsey!" said Mom.

"Oh, come off it, Mom! She dresses like she's a nun, her new haircut makes her look like a lesbian, aka Justin Bieber, and she has no clue that we are in twenty fourteen."

Ouch, that hurt, but she was right. I looked at myself and also my family. I remembered my friends and what they said and how they acted and looked. I was stuck in a time where people met their mates at college and in libraries. I needed to snap out of it. So I said thanks, smiled, did a fake yawn, and asked my dad to take me home.

"Oh your sleepy? Well my dear get some rest, love you"

"I love you too mom" I gave everyone a kiss and a hug before leaving. I looked at dad and grabbed my coat. Slumping into his passenger seat I took a deep breath.

"Well, sweetie, was it that bad?"

"Worse than what it looked like, Dad. Dinner was a nightmare."

"So what's this deal with this Bang thing?"

"Well my friends don't want me to die alone, remember? And I don't have any social networking site, and they insist it's a great way to get out of my shell."

"What do you think?"

"Well, Dad, I don't know. I'm in my thirties, lonely, and work a dead-end job. I don't take risks and try new things. I'm in my bubble, and this bubble is about to pop."

"Well, love, you don't need a fake profile picture or tons of friends to be loved. Sure, it isn't the love of a man, but hey, we love you. Just be you. He will come, honey. Be patient."

Before I knew it, I was kissing my dad goodnight and walking up the stairs to my apartment. I slowly made my way to my room and plopped down on my bed. I kicked off my shoes and very lazily peeled off my clothes. I walked to the shower in my birthday suit and sat in the tub for about two hours. I realized that my life was on hold, at a standstill, and I had no one else to blame but me. I wasn't up to date on anything in this century, especially romance. It was time for a change! I jumped up from sulking in the tub, slipped and hit my head, but realized it was time for a makeover.

* * *

S'up, Diary,

Well today din-din with the fam-bam didn't go so hot. They informed me that I am in fact a lame tard and that I look like a 70-year-old lesbian nun. So I've decided that they are right and it's time for a makeover. Lord, please be with me because I will need the help of Jen and the rest of my friends. Off to bed! I have to see Ursula tomorrow, aka Kelly <3 Hope

Ugh

I got up that morning after dinner a little uneasy. I'd thought I was okay, I'd thought I looked good, and I'd thought I was up to date. Supposedly what I'd thought was completely wrong. I was feeling extremely sluggish and decided to reach over to my phone and shoot Kelly a little text:

"Hey Kelly, I will be in late today. This morning is not going well, I need to take time to regroup"

As I walked to the bathroom I decided to take a bath instead of a shower today. I soaked in the tub and tried to rest my eyes as I let the hot water rest on my skin. As soon as I was in relaxation paradise, my phone dinged. I reached over and unwilling picked it up. To my surprise, it was Kelly. Hadn't thought she would be up this early.

"Hey non-Bang fried. Yeah I guess that's okay, seems like you need someone to pick up where Hank left off? Oh well, too bad. I guess I'll see you when you get in slacker. Oh and By the way, pick me up some coffee, you know how I like it."

I tried my best not to slam my phone; she was such an idiot! So now that I was out of Zen, time to refocus. I got back to soaking, grabbing my Dove bubbles. Right when I reached my relaxation moment, someone decided to knock on my door. I waited awhile to see if they would leave or if Jen would get the door, but of course not. Why would anyone leave me alone when I needed to be left alone?

"I'm coming!" I yelled as I jumped out of the tub and walked as slowly as I could to the door. I looked up and asked God why and if he was just playing a joke on me. Since I got no response, I decided to answer the door anyway.

"S'up, Athena."

"Sean, what the hell, it's seven in the morning."

"Actually it's seven-oh-one in the morning."

"Shut up, what do you want?"

"I'm here to make things all better!"

"Like…"

"Like hook your Bang up to your phone so that you can get notifications when someone wants to communicate with you.'

"And why would I want to be that accessible?"

"Remember, because you're like fifty and your eggs are dead."

"Ahh, oh yeah, that's right. And I'm thirty-two. And why does my age always go up when we talk about my eggs?"

"Because it does. Now move out the way. Hand me your cellular communication device and laptop."

I did exactly what my early bird friend insisted as he went into the kitchen to raid my fridge. "Thanks, now go finish relaxing and allow King of Arizona Computers to set you up." I couldn't help but roll my eyes at him and walked back to my probably cold bath.

About twenty minutes later, Sean came into the bathroom, sat on the toilet seat, and decided to talk to me. He pulled up my computer screen and showed me what he'd done. Honestly, I didn't care. I could hardly remember what he'd said at the door.

"So now you are officially reachable."

"Thanks."

"Anytime, Athena."

"So I didn't know it takes that long to hook things up like that."

"Oh, it doesn't. I had it done about five minutes after you gave me your phone."

"So what were you doing?"

"Oh, reading through your messages."

"What?"

"Your MESSAGES! M-E-S-S—"

"I know what you said, ass face, I mean 'what' as in 'I have messages?'"

"Yup, quite a few from some guys. They seem weird. Well anyway, enjoy your dirt soak. I'm off to work."

He left the bathroom door wide open while slurping a damn slushie. I looked at my phone and realized what time it was. I'd told Kelly I was going to be a little late, not almost a couple hours late. I jumped out of the tub, threw on some clothes, and headed into work. Man, today was going to be a long day.

Work. It's such a non-pleasant place to be. I got to

my desk and slumped deep down into my very uncomfortable chair. I reluctantly hit the spacebar on my keyboard and waited for my computer to wake up. I logged onto my company email and went through my agenda like normal. Kelly had sent us all an email on how there was a mandatory meeting at nine a.m., and the email ended with a winking smiley face. Great. The clock that said eight fifty-five a.m., so I decided to waste some time by checking my Bang. I click my friend requests and, to my surprise, Kelly had added me as a friend. I didn't accept it right away because, well, she's a douche, my boss, and a douchey boss. So I clicked into my messages and saw that someone had sent me a message. It was a guy named Richie Stint. He was tan, seemed to be tall, and spoke three languages, according to his profile. I browsed his page some more before I accepted his request or replied to his message. He seemed pretty impressive, so I decided to read what he had written.

> *Hey, My name is Richie. I came across your picture and I think that you are gorgeous. I just had to tell you that. Have a good day today. I would love to hear from you but I understand that you may get that a lot from guys on here. Anyway have a good day (again).*
> *-Richie*

Hmmm, he seemed interesting enough for me to respond to. I

reread his message a couple more times and was about to write back when Kelly popped up.

"Hey, bitch!"

"Kelly, oh hi, I didn't see you. How are you?"

"Yeah, whatevs. Sooo I sent you a FR on the B and you didn't accept."

"Oh, really? I must not have seen it. Hmmm, I'm sorry."

"Um, don't lie, heifer, I saw you on there. I was watching you type. That Richie is a real sweet talker, huh? Well, anywizzay! Meeting starts, like, now, and you're late."

"Well you're late, too."

"I'm never late, I'm the boss."

I rolled my eyes at her and continued to type my response to Richie before I followed the smell of Brittney Spears perfume into the conference room. We spent a total of an hour and 30 minutes discussing this new paper company that had just planted its feet next door. Kelly had a pretty good idea about trying to buddy up some packages to sell. Since they were a paper company and since we sold pens, maybe both companies could come together for an awesome package deal. Kelly then divided us into two groups. One was to make a presentation on the pros of working together, and the other group was to create a mission statement. This was all to be done professionally. Even though she had a great idea, she still treated us like babies.

"Alrighty, guys, let's get into our groups and work the rest of the day. The meeting will be on Friday! Bring your A-game, your best shit and all that hoopla!"

We broke off into our groups and started to plan something spectacular to get the other guys to join forces. Would it be wrong for me to say that my team was sure to win because I was on it? Well if you said yes, screw you, I love myself! We worked for the majority of the day until we got sick of seeing each other. We decided to go back to our desks and work on our other projects and reunite tomorrow.

I walked slowly but surely to my desk, a little beat because I was paired with the one who smelled like ketchup and the armpit smeller. Who would've thought that the people who weren't paying attention would have the most questions? Right when I sat down I got interrupted by big boobs.

"Hey, Hope. Hope, who won't be my friend or send back a slap."

"Oh, hi, Kelly."

"Accept me!"

Ugh, is she serious? Yeah, that is not happening. I

smiled and glared, then put on a fake laugh. She giggled too and skipped away from my desk. I slammed my head down, hitting my forehead on the space bar. My computer screen lit up; I couldn't believe I'd forgotten to log out of my Bang. So I refreshed my page and, as I pointed my mouse to the upper right-hand corner, I noticed I'd gotten another message. So before I decided to go home for the day, I checked it out.

Wow, I didn't think you would have time to write me back! Well I am very glad that you did. I read your profile too and I like your display picture. I won't be surprised if you have a boyfriend. If you do, tell him I'm sorry for coming onto you. ☺

I couldn't help but smile. I perked up my boobs, flung my hair like Kelly, and did a disgusting giggle. I turned red and got about a billion butterflies in my stomach. It didn't seem like it would be a bad day at all.

As a matter of fact, it seemed like it was going to be a good day. Funny how just one thing can cause you to smile and change your attitude.

At midday the next day, Kelly called an emergency meeting. She sent out an email stating work conduct and harassment policies in the workplace. *This should be good, seeing how Kelly is the one who smacks everyone on their butts and calls us "sexies" instead of our real names.*

Heading towards the conference room, everyone seemed so confused and started to chitchat amongst each other, whispering things like, "I wonder what this is about," and "Is she firing someone again but sugarcoating it?"

"What up, bitches! So like I said in the memo, today is about conduct and sexual harassment in the workplace! So I've been getting a few anonymous emails from someone about another someone giving them the googly eyes. And apparently this makes someone very nervous. So with that being said! HERE ARE THE RULES, HOES! One, no one smacks asses but me. Two, no eyes, just look down. And three, smile. Meeting adjourned."

Now that was the most ridiculous time-wasting meeting ever! I refused to allow that to ruin my mood, especially after my positive message from Richie. The rest of the week went by smoothly. Got a few messages from the buds and my dad, checking in on me. I thought I'd keep this one quiet for awhile; didn't want to speak too soon.

* * *

Hey Diary,

Funny thing, I don't hate Bang as much as I thought I would. Someone really likes me. He's handsome and has an impressive profile. Not going to think too much of it since it is online. Is that wrong? Anyways I hate to say it but I think my friends are onto something here. Maybe this social networking stuff isn't too bad. I mean guys are messaging me and that's never happened before. Anywho time to get some sleep. Goodnight.

<3 Becoming an Optimist Hope ☺

Feeling Kinda Good

So a couple weeks went by, and Richie and I were Bang messaging every day. I got to know him pretty well, and he seemed to take an interest in me. About maybe a month into Banging I decided to give him my number. He did the gentlemanly thing and waited a couple days to text me. He said he didn't want to rush things or seem too excited; little did he know those were the words I wanted to hear.

I woke up one morning and did the usual routine, but this time I inserted some love songs, mainly by Barry White and Brian McKnight. I checked my Bang account and had a lot more friend requests and messages. I still had the request from Kelly sitting in my inbox; I didn't get why she didn't understand that no means just that: NO!

After my bathroom time, I sent Richie a good morning text. This morning seemed really odd since I hadn't heard Jen. I looked in her room, and nothing. Then in the kitchen, and nope, no food out. The television was turned off, and when I looked outside her car was gone. I hoped she was okay. Had I really passed out, neglecting to notice that she'd never come home? Right when I was in deep thought I got a random text from Jen. She said she wouldn't be home until late and that life is like a box of over-dried chocolates and that you never know what you're gonna get. I translated that to mean that something drastic had happened and she wanted to drink and be alone. I tried to text her back but I didn't get a response. Now she was making me pretty damn nervous; I hoped she wouldn't go out and do something stupid. Again.

Since Jen wasn't coming home tonight that left just me and the boys for game night. I started to clean, got some snacks, and made the table. Soon enough the doorbell rang; it was a great day and nothing could ruin it.

"ATHENA!" yelled Sean.

"Hope! Ya lover boys are here!" said Ray.

"So answer the door, you dirty girl, you!" said Sean.

"We got those chains and clamps you wanted!" yelled Ray.

"Yeah, and the jelly! You liked man musk for the

scent, right?" asked Sean.

I ran as fast as I could to the door. My two doofus friends *would* make me look like a hoochie in front of my stuffy neighbors just because they think it's funny. I opened the door, grabbed the two of them by the jackets, yanked them in, and apologized to Ms. Delaney. She's my next-door neighbor who always walks her dog at night and stares at everyone and everything.

"S'up, Athena, where's my boo?"

"Well read this." I showed them the message she'd sent and they didn't seem too surprised. Apparently Jen had been having some guy trouble lately. And from the look on their faces, he'd probably dumped her.

"So, I will take a wild guess and say that she is not coming tonight?"

"Good observation, cement arms."

"Yeah, Ray, she's not coming," I said.

"Damn! I hate when these retards hurt my boo."

"Y'all aren't even a couple," said Ray.

"Yet. Not a couple yet."

Since it was supposed to be game night, we decided to watch a movie instead; it's hard to play a game with three people when I only have games for four or more. Soon it was midnight and we'd gone through five bags of popcorn, a couple of hot dogs, and a box of popsicles.

"So, Hope, do you still talk to this Richie guy?" asked Ray.

"As of matter of fact I do, and I gave him my number."

"WHAT?! Someone stepped into the real world!" yelled Sean.

"Yeah, yeah, I know! He seems genuine, and right when I was questioning the male species, here Richie comes. And he's more interested in my brain than body."

"That's because he hasn't seen you in person yet!"

"Yeah, so when's the date?" asked Sean.

"Date?"

"Yeah. Date, ATHENA! You've been 'talking' for about a month or so now."

"I know, and I just gave him my number,"

"Define 'just?'" asked Ray.

"A couple days ago?" I replied.

"WHAT?!" they said in unison.

"Yo, he's gay," said Ray.

"What? No he's not."

"What man waits a couple months for a number!?" asked Sean

"A respectful one!"

"OR, one that has other women," said Ray.

"Or he's gay," said Sean.

"Shut up! Movie is about to start."

"What is this shit anyways?" asked Sean.

"*Cry Baby*," I said.

"*Cry Baby*? The Johnny Depp one?" Sean asked.

"Yes."

"DEAR GOD! Do you have any movies that aren't depressing and that are from this century, Athena?"

"Shhhh, it's starting!" said Ray.

About four movies in, my thoughts were heavy on the possibility that Richie might have a girlfriend or be gay. I looked over to see Sean asleep, with popcorn on his shirt and a popsicle in his mouth, as was Ray, who was spread out on my recliner with a beer in his hand. *So I can assume movie night is over.* I began to clean up quietly and turned the volume down.

Before going to bed I texted Jen, letting her know I loved her and was here if she needed me. I jumped into bed and checked my Bang app. I had two more friend requests and a few messages. Someone named Mel had written: *Hey I like your puddy cat.*

Alvin said: *Man I have the same cat, maybe ours can play together soon.*

75

George said: *hey, I like you, let's forget this site and really bang.*

Oh yeah, and did I mention I had about eight slaps from guys who had cats as their display picture too?

* * *

Diary!! My beezy!

So the night went alright. It would've been better if we'd had our firecracker Jen with us. I hope she's okay. She has me worried; she usually comes to me with things. I don't like being up in the winds with things. Sean and Ray can't be right, right? I mean, Richie isn't gay, he's totally into me! And he def doesn't have a girlfriend because, well, he's into me! I just hope Thing One and Thing Two are wrong....
Anyways, time to sleep!
<3 The Heavy-Minded Hop

Mystery Guy

I didn't have the greatest night's sleep since I had no idea where Jen was. I tossed and turned and got woken up several times by this random cat and my roommate. I had a really awkward dream about this makeover. I'd all of a sudden become fabulous and moved in with Kim Kardashian and slept with Kanye West. Khloé found out and then decided to kick my ass; this girl in my dream was huge! So of course after she knocked me out I woke up. Talk about a nightmare. Now as for this damn cat, I swear if I didn't donate to PETA I would seriously kick the living daylights outta Garfield.

I staggered to my bathroom, passing Jen's room along the way. I heard some noises so I decided to stick my ear to the door. I couldn't make out the sounds completely, but it sounded like a wounded horse making love to a tiny elephant on bubble wrap. Aka Jen was getting some. I still haven't figured out which noises are hers because with every guy it sounds the same. Hmm, maybe she's making both noises at the same time? Talk about talent.

I jumped in the shower and sang Pat Benatar's "Hit Me With Your Best Shot" as loud as I could. I used my back

77

scrubber as the mic, and my body soap bubbles were my adoring fans. I turned around and showed some love to the fans up top, aka my shampoo and conditioner bottles, and then sang down low to the faucet and drain. Oh yeah, I am a natural. Before I knew it, *BAM*! The door opened and someone ran in sat on Mr. Hanky (yeah, I named the toilet after my ex). I slid the curtains open and wasn't surprised by what I saw. It was Jen, a little drunk, makeup running, pooping everywhere. It was like she was possessed and the multiple demons were trying to come out. To my surprise, it was Thursday; I wasn't expecting this for another two days or so.

"Hey, sexy," I said, trying not to laugh.

"S'up."

"So, long night?"

"Kinda, still haven't been to sleep."

"What's wrong?"

"Remember that guy I told you about? The one I had a date with?"

"Yes, the one you nicknamed Dick."

"Well, that was last night."

"YAY! So how did that go?" As I asked, here came some random Asian guy. I gave Jen a look, hoping this wasn't Mr. Sexy that she said she'd had a date with.

"Well, this isn't the guy."

"That bad, huh? "

"Man, so he stood me up. Ignored my texts and calls. So I met Juan here—"

"Juan? He's Asian."

"Oh, well, I don't remember, I just call him Juan and he answers. So anyways, I met him, we drank, freaked, and now we are here. All in the personal space, in the bathroom—"

"So wait! Why stand you up!?"

"Well, I saw him texting during our last hangout, and it was to some girl, called her 'The Plan for Hope,' and he's nonstop texting! I know he has a huge project that he's working on for work so I understand the importance of those texts. Long story short, I made a big fuss about it and he left, and then he was a no-show."

"Damn, Jen, I'm so sorry to hear that. Want me to call in today and we can have some girl time?"

"No, you need to go and make Kelly's life hell like usual. Don't forget her coffee!"

"Oh, shut up! Haha! But okay, if you need me I'm a text or call away. Love you, girl!"

"Ew, don't be gay!"

I left for work even though my gut was telling me to

stay with Jen. But she was a big girl and could talk to me anytime. By the way, the bathroom smelled so bad! Just FYI.

I finally got to work, a little late, and I forgot the demon's coffee. I tried to sneak to my desk but for some reason everyone—and I mean EVERYONE—wanted to say hi to me, and believe me, those doofs were not quiet about it. I'd almost made it to my desk when the wicked witch made eye contact with me and started to walk my way.

"Oh, hello, person who won't add me and obviously forgot my coffee!"

"Oh, hey, you! I was just.... You know what--"

"Save it, Hope, I would like to see you in my office in ten! Okay?"

"Ten what? Minutes?"

"Well, I mean—"

"Or seconds? Hours? Breaths? Kels, you have to be specific now."

"Damn it, Hope! Don't confuse me when it's so early in the morning!"

"It's nine thirty."

"Ugh, stop reminding me!"

"Whatever. I'll see you in ten, Kelly."

"Okay, so ten as in...?"

"Seriously?"

"No, not seriously, silly!" Kelly said as she laughed and hit me on the shoulder. She walked back to her office and picked up her phone. *BUZZ.* My phone's speaker went off. I knew who it was. I looked behind me and saw Kelly pointing for me to pick up my phone.

"Yeah, Kelly."

"So just come now because I can't wait ten hours."

For the love of humanity, how is she running this company? Was she really going to sit there for ten hours? Ugh, who was I kidding? She probably would have. Slowly walking into her office, I had my head thrown back and was walking as if I were a zombie.

"Ew, don't do that!"

"Don't do what, Kelly?"

"That thing with your body, it's gross."

"You mean walk like this?" I stuck my arms out and began to walk like Frankenstein, making very gross, creepy noises.

"Yes, like that! Cut it out! So here's the deal, we need to be friends."

"Kelly, not the Bang thing again."

"No, I'm upping the game. I'm talking about in real life."

An awkward silence filled the room while Kelly

smiled and stared into my soul, slowly sucking it out. I wanted to throw up.

"In real life? How is this work-related or appropriate?"

"It's not, but I'm the boss so I can do what I want. No, seriously, I believe we can work together and help each other in way more ways than known to man."

"Kelly, I don't get down like that."

"Like what?"

"You know, the girl-on-girl thing. That's not me."

"Ew, no, but really it isn't? I mean, by your haircut and how you're letting it grow out I would've guessed otherwise.

"Why does everyone think I'm a lesbian?"

"Because you are, and anyways, no, seriously, we can totally help each other out. I can teach you some things with the business and how to be attractive, and you can teach me how to ummm be more reserved?"

"Why are you wanting to do this?"

"Remember when I was out for that stomachache?"

"Yeah."

"Well, I had a meeting with Daddy, and you're the only go-to person for this, so don't tell anyone."

"Okay, Kelly, you're making me nervous."

"Well, Daddy said Sharps has gone under ever since he took the business from my brother to me. Can you believe that?"

"Yes, I can."

"Shut up. Anyways I need a new strategy, a new plan, a partner. I need help, and you're the smartest person here who is semi-attractive. There will be a big deal coming soon that I need to close. I have to, to save all of our asses. I would like your help with this client. They are a billion-dollar company, and that means you get your cut on whatever contract they choose to buy. The meeting will be in a couple weeks to a month, depends on when they come from Japan. Are you down?"

"Damn, Kelly, this is a lot to take in, I will have to check on that and think about it. I'll get back to you."

"Okay, just don't take too long. And Hope, don't tell anyone, k?"

"Promise."

I walked away and closed Kelly's office door behind me. Everyone was staring into the office and at my face, trying to figure out what went on. I'd gotten to my desk and put my head down when I started to feel a vibration. My phone was going off like crazy. It was Jen, who said she could really use some Hope time. Really? Right now, after

I'd gotten all that news and had a lot to think on? Of course! Why not. I picked up my phone and buzzed into Kelly's office.

"Hey, Kelly, Jen really needs me. I'm going to take off the rest of the day."

"Only if you promise to use some of that time to think about what I just said."

"Deal."

"Okay, see you tomorrow."

I gathered my things and headed out of Sharps. Getting into my car, I couldn't help but think about Kelly's offer and what Jen was going through. Pulling up to the house, I could see Jen in the window doing the Insanity Workout. When I walked into the house, the television was on full-blast and she was crying and sweating. So much wetness in one room made me sick.

"Hey there!"

"Oh, hey, Hope, I'm almost done."

"I see that."

"So here's the deal, Hope!

One...two...three...four...PUSH! Ok, sorry. I get a new outfit, get my hair done—three...four...five...kick—and then I want to glam up and go to a bar—

seven...eight...nine...DONE! Phew. So how does that sound?"

"Honestly, I'm a little terrified but that sounds great."

"Okay, awesome. I'll get fresh, be out in twenty."

I sat on the couch, disinfected the remotes and anything else her sweat touched, turned off the workout tape, and waited for Jen to be ready. When twenty minutes had passed Jen was smiling and ready. We jumped into her car and headed straight for the mall. As we took forever to find a parking space we bobbed our heads to Michael Jackson.

"Ok, so tell me more about this guy, Jen."

"Well, we met on Bang and had been talking for quite some time. I kept him quiet because I wasn't sure. We hit it off, hit everything off, actually. He's tall, smart, brown hair, successful and no kids, and loves life. He seemed like the one. We'd been on many dates, had great nights and laughs. Then all of a sudden for the past month or so he's been distant and just left me. Felt like I was a project or a placeholder."

"Wow, Jen, I'm upset also. I can't believe he would do that. Drag you through all of that to just peace out. Well, sucks for him. Let's get you a makeover and get another one!"

"Do you want a makeover? That lesbian hair isn't workin' for me anymore."

"No, not yet. I still love me right now, and plus today is Jen's day."

We spent the rest of the day glamming Jen up, making her smile, and watching movies. I love when my bestie is okay, and I hate the men who make it so she's not. In the middle of our day, Jen got a text from Dick that seemed to kind of change the mood .

"Look what he said, Hope: 'Hey Jen I'm sorry love, please forgive me, are you free tonight?'"

"Well, Jen, are you?"

"I am, but not for him. But anyways I got to get out of here. Promised the fam I would do movie night with them. Drop me off at home?"

"Ok, cool."

As we walked to the car, continuously talking about Dick and Jen and her newfound woman power, I was inspired. Rolling up to the house, Jen told me she wouldn't be home and that she was staying at her parents' house.

Walking into the house, I plopped on the couch and kicked off my shoes and was taking a deep breath when I heard a voice.

"Long day, Athena?"

"Sean?"

"Yeah, let myself in."

"Ugh, what are you doing here?"

"I can't find arms and didn't want to be alone tonight. He has a hot date and I'm having nightmares."

"Sean, you're a grown-ass man."

"And those nightmares are grown as hell, so what do you say? Slumber party?"

"Ugh, fine!"

In the middle of my bath I got a text from Jen, saying, *I'm stupid and fell into the trap!* After trying to text her back and call, I got no answer. I was betting she'd seen Dick and was thrown for a loop.

* * *

Dear Diary,

I hope Jen will be okay and I pray God watches her. Also I need to get better locks on my doors! Goodnight.
<3 The Exhausted Hope

Ebony Williams

The Gym is NOT a Place for Jen Right Now

After a very uplifting day, my week seemed to go by hella fast. It was now Friday, and I was headed to the gym. Work had been a little rough; Kelly kept staring at me, trying to figure out if I'd made my decision about whether I would help save the day for Sharps. I know most people would jump on the opportunity, but Kelly is so evil and always has something up her sleeve; I didn't know if I could or even wanted to trust her. I still hadn't seen or talked to Jen, and Richie and I were moving pretty fast, so I had lots to think about. As I walked into the gym I decided to let this place be the place to hash out my emotions. So I walked in all happy and smiley, ready to bust a sweat. I thought I was in a bad, confused mood? Well, walking into the gym and feeling that aura made me realize that today everyone was in a bad mood.

I walked over to the treadmill and noticed that everyone was either zoned into the TV or trying to outrun each other. It brought back memories of losing my hair. On the weights, old men tried to squat more than the young bodybuilders, and in the stretching area, people were actually stretching. There were few conversations going on, and when I thought about it, I hadn't been harassed by Ted the check-in guy. As I revved up the treadmill, I saw Jen with a client. I waved vigorously, trying to get her attention. I assumed that she'd had a bad day because she was eating a donut, wearing sweats that were not color-coordinating, and yelling at this 16-year-old girl to "Push! And if you cry, no one will hear you!" Yeah, we were gonna have to talk about that later.

There were way too many distractions for me to try and run at that moment, so I headed over to the stretching area. Once I got there, I looked to the right of me and saw two Barbies arguing over five-pound dumbbells. To the left, muscle heads were beating their chests and doing squats. Questions? What's up with buff people being OVERLY loud at the gym? Okay, for ONE, we definitely see you with all those damn muscles so WHY must you grunt?

Despite the entertainment and bitchiness at the gym, I ignored the rudeness and put on my headphones, walked back to the treadmill, and started to jog. On the TV was a story about this guy who was a serial leg-sniffer. He apparently found girls on social networking sites and sniffed their legs against their will. This was a new form of harassment and apparently this is what our world is coming to.

After my 30-minute run, I walked towards the locker room to get my sweats and leave the gym. My BFF finally saw me and waved; she also mouthed, *I need to talk to you.* I

nodded and smiled and said, "See you at home." This was
going to be interesting; at least I had a few hours to relax
before hearing the shitstorm from Jen.

At home I turned on the TV, began stretching, and
waited patiently for Jen to come home. I was so lazy I left it
on the channel it was already on. I guessed Jen was really
going through something; she never watches Lifetime, and
when I turned on the TV it was on that channel. Lifetime is a
getaway for us females to watch other females be crazy and
do things to men and their families that we would LOVE to
do. But instead we don't because we don't want to rot in
prison.

The movie was called *To Kill a Babysitter*. From the
title I took a wild guess that this was about a man who cheats
on his wife and she in return kills both of them. *Fingers
crossed, I think I may be right!* Before I knew it I was sucked
into this ridiculous movie and forgot all about stretching.
There was a huge twist at the end: Supposedly the babysitter
wanted the husband, but he refused, so she went for the wife,
who couldn't refuse. In the end the husband killed the
babysitter and chained up his wife, only to be found by their
daughter! Man, this was stupid and intense. The acting was
horrible, but yet you couldn't stop watching. Oh, Lifetime,
thank you for wasting an hour and 45 minutes of my life and

possibly being the reason for me getting terrible cramps since I forgot to stretch.

Being a little pissy at the fact that I had watched this movie, I got up slowly to grab some water. Jen came storming in the house. She threw down her gym bag, singing her heart out to Lady Gaga, went to the fridge, grabbed some ice cream, sat on the couch (totally bombarding my space), put in a movie (even though I was watching Lifetime), popped in *Flash Dance*, and then—wait for it—started crying. In the midst of all this, I was looking at her, a little scared because when Jen keeps walking NEVER, and I mean NEVER, get in her way. I walked over to the couch, sat down with extreme caution, grabbed the remote from her gorilla-grip hands, and put the movie on pause. I feared for my life a little bit because she looked like a rabid rabbit on steroids with a mouth full of ice cream or foam, whatever you prefer to use.

"Hey, fatty. Soooo how was your day?" She glared at me, chewed slowly, and turned her focus back to the television. "Okay, the silent treatment. Perfect. Exactly what I want from my friend who is making a mess on our nice, brand new couch. So, no talking, huh? Well then I will go on and tell you about my exciting day at the office! First—"

"Okay! Wait."

I knew Jen couldn't stand hearing about my days at Sharps, Inc.

"So remember that guy I wanted you to meet? Dick? Well, he dumped me!"

"WHAT! Why?! I thought he already did that?"

"Well, yeah, but remember I went to my mom's for movie night? Well he texted me, so I met up with him. We had sex and had a great sleep. Then I woke up and...I have no idea! He said we are in two different places in our lives and it doesn't seem right. He wants to focus on school again and do a program in India to help some of the needy kids."

"Oh, Jen, love, that's not bad! Maybe when he gets back ya'll can be together again?"

"Maybe. He is leaving me to be with some snot-nosed kids!"

"Ooookaaaay, well he is leaving you because he wants to help people who don't get the attention they should receive."

"Same diff."

"Yeah, okay, so let's keep eating ice cream and watch *Flash Dance*. Tomorrow this will all make sense in your mind and you will be okay."

I couldn't help but laugh on the inside at her interpretation of what Dick was doing. We watched the movie about three times before Jen remembered that I had something to tell her too.

"Hey, so what did you want to tell me?"

"Oh, you mean besides wanting to know why you made a sixteen-year-old prep cheerleader cry today?"

"HA! She will be okay! She needs tough love, she won't be cute forever."

"Okay, so if you don't know, meanie sucks face, you're kind of rude today."

"What's new?"

"This is true. Okay, so I decided to change."

"As in what?"

"Myself. Well, not myself, per se, but my look."

"I'm listening, keep talking."

My phone went off in the middle of our conversation. I couldn't help but look to see if it was Richie; instead it was a text from Bang, saying I'd gotten a new message. As I went to check it, I was interrupted by Jen.

"Umm, HELLO! Ms. Cell Phone!"

"Oh yeah, sorry. I want a makeover."

"I peed a little."

"And I want you to help me with it."

"Mama has never been happier!"

She hugged me with a smile, then began to cry again.

Oh boy, this was going to be not only a long-ass night but a long process to make me over. I couldn't find the strength to tell her that I wanted to get all dolled up for Richie. Mainly because I didn't want her to know that she was right; social networking wasn't that bad. Now one question: Is it safe to say I was a little scared?

"Okay, so when do you want to start? Can I tell the guys?"

"No, don't tell the guys just yet, but as soon as we can, I'm ready to be modernized."

"AH! I love you! And how about this weekend?!"

"Okay, that sounds good to me."

"Great, now push play."

* * *

Dear Diary,

So I asked Jen for help. Seemed to get her out of her funk. Now I just need baby Jesus in this. Please don't let me turn into a bimbo.

<3 Keeping My Fingers Crossed I'll Recognize Who I am After This Hope

Let it Begin

"Wait…. You mean Hope? Our Hope?" said Ray.

"Athena Hope?" said Sean.

"Our precious, out-of-the-loop Hope—" chimed in Ray.

"Wants a makeover?" asked Sean.

"Yes, boys, this is true," Jen said while smiling.

"And she wants you—" Ray went on.

"To…um, fix her up?" questioned Sean.

"Yeah! And?!" said Jen as she started to get a little mad.

Both Ray and Sean busted out in a high-pitched laugh, followed by tears and some high-fiving. Jen couldn't do anything but sit back and watch as the two playfully joked around.

"Yeah, she wants me, dipsticks! What's so bad about that?" They looked at each other, back at Jen, and then to each other again and started laughing.

"Okay, here's the thing," said Ray. "You really don't have style."

"Excuse me!"

"Muscles is right, boo thang. You just dress like a

whore," joked Sean.

"UGH! RUDE!"

"And yet very true, my blond nibblet," said Ray.

"Well, whatever, you two freak tards! Play your dumb game. I'm gonna hop in the shower and prep myself. Hope is coming back from work soon and we are going shopping."

"Good luck with that, sweet face."

"Whatever, geek brain."

"At least I have a brain!"

"I do too!"

"Yeah, two big ones!!" laughed Ray.

"Good one, muscle skull!"

As the boys laughed and high-fived, Jen walked over to the game system and pulled the plug.   "Now who's laughing!" she said as she walked away smiling.

Today at work sucked big time. It was Friday, and that meant that we had to present to Kelly our mission statements and PowerPoints on why our paper neighbors should join forces with Sharps, Inc. In the middle of my presentation and saying my kick-ass mission statement, Miss Ketchup Hands decided that she wanted to sneeze and fart at the same time. I know that doesn't sound too bad, but she also soiled herself, therefore causing us to reschedule.

Kelly is as dramatic as they come. She screamed and pretended to throw up. In my head I was saying, *So now you have bad gag reflexes? Man what am I going to do with her? She is a hot mess in a plastic body; I'm surprised she hasn't melted by now.*

We all grabbed our stuff and walked out as quickly as we could. Since we were the last to present, that meant the day was over! I skipped to my desk, sat down, and started to pack all my stuff. As soon as I popped my head up, BAM! There she was.

"Hey, Hope."

"Hey, Kelly."

"Sooo, Bang me!"

"Excuse me?"

"Girl! Accept my friend request! I see future BFFs on the way."

She flipped her hair and strutted her nonexistent ass away from my desk. I laughed while staring at my Bang friend requests and reluctantly accepted. Jumping into the car, I blasted "Boom Boom Pow" by the Black Eyed Peas and headed home. TGIF, and tonight the makeover would begin.

I walk into the house to what seemed like World War III, but considering how Jen was screaming, I should change that to a WWE match. Just so you know what I'm talking about and why my friends are a bunch of doofus brains, this is what I walked in on.

We had Ray muscle bags sitting on Jen while Sean was poking her with the XBOX controller. Jen was screaming, "Ahh, I hate you guys!" Ray was laughing and Sean was saying, "Never mess with *Call of Duty*! EVER!" Yeah, my three big kids. Tonight maybe wasn't going to be a getaway after all.

"Hey, guys!" I shouted.

"Yo, ATHENA! What up?"

"So, I hate to interrupt, but what ya doin' to Jen?"

"Well, she rejected my love again, so we have muscles sitting on her until she agrees to marry me."

"Yeah! Whatever, Abu! Eat monkey turds and get off of me, you sack of nonexistent fat!"

"Hey, guys, so you may not remember, but I need Jen to make me sexy, so Ray, up, and Sean, put that damn controller down."

Jen jumped up and smacked Ray and Sean then ran behind me. She got herself together and smiled while sticking out her tongue at the boys.

"So, hot face, you ready to do this?"

"Yup!"

"Alright, let's go to the mall!"

"So, I have some car ride discussion!"

"Oooh, Jen like!"

"Must you talk about yourself in third person?"

"Affirmative."

"Okay, you have been hanging with Sean WAY too much. Well, anywho, there is a guy."

"Hmm, a male guy?"

"Umm, yeah. Anyway, I like him, and we may have a date soon."

"You may have a date?"

"Yeah, he hasn't asked yet, but I'm pretty sure that it will happen."

"Is that confidence Jen hears? Jen like! Now it's time to make this transformation even more awesome!"

There we were in Jen's car, blasting music and singing along like we were teenagers and heading downtown. The whole ride to the mall, Jen and I were giggling and talking about boys. She told me her guy, named Richard, had finally left for Africa and they'd had one big SHEBANG before he left. She seemed okay with it, but honestly I felt like it tore her up. She'd actually allowed herself to catch feelings for this guy. I went on to tell her about Richie from Bang and how we've been in contact almost 24/7. I didn't have the heart to tell her that the guys knew more than she did.

"So is that why you are glued to your phone now?"

"No, not because of Richie."

"Then why?"

"Well, because, I guess, it's just the fact that I am finally into society and I feel wanted. Kelly sent me a request, and ever since I changed my cat picture I've been getting tons of messages and slaps from some guys. It's definitely helping my confidence."

"Well that's good, I guess."

"Why do you sound unsure?"

"Well because, I see you changing a little."

"In a bad way?"

"No, not really."

"Then what's the big deal? This was your guys' idea to get Hope into reality, remember?"

"You're right, maybe I'm trippin'. Ok, let's-"

Before she could finish her sentence, we walked into this weird guy. He stood there and stared for a little bit, then finally spoke.

"S'up," random citizen said.

"Hey?" I said.

"What you want, freak face?" asked Jen.

"This is my friend."

"Who?" Jen and I said.

"Her," as he pointed to me.

"Hmm, and how so?" said Jen.

"Bang."

"Whoa! Ya'll banged?!" Jen said.

"I wish!"

"Um, not happening, Gollum."

"Well, okay, we didn't bang and we aren't exactly Bang friends, even though we should be." As he sipped his drink, I got caught in a trance. Staring into his face I realized who it was!

"Trent?"

"Ah ha! I knew you knew who I was! See? It's destiny!"

"Yeah, it's not you're just creepy."

"Oh you're the Bang stalker. Yeah, beat it, freak face."

"But, Hope...I–"

"If you yell you love me I will demolish you."

Jen and I walked away from random weirdo and went on with our previous conversation. We went into Nordstrom, and Jen had me trying on everything from a sophisticated

First Lady dress to something not so classy—try a grunge, holey tights-wearing emo outfit. She seemed to get a kick out of it. We walked the isles looking at some of the things on the racks. Jen pulled out this horrendous bright pink sweater. It cut open in the front and had bright pink feathers along the collar and wrists.

"Are you serious? We are NOT in the movie *Clueless*!" I said.

Jen busted out laughing and decided to put on the sweater as we walked throughout the store. To my surprise, Nordstrom had nothing, so we left and headed down the hall to this cute boutique. The name was NES Fashions, and the display window was amazing! On the manikin was this black dress with some tiger print for the skirt and for the bra area. To the left, the other manikin was wearing this drop-dead gorgeous red dress. Jen kept walking, but I was stunned. I had to go in. Soon Jen realized she'd lost me and backtracked to NES Fashions. Jen picked up a pair of jeans that had a Scorpio symbol imprinted on the back pocket. I walked towards another rack and picked up this navy blue dress that had a red belt. I grabbed it off the rack and looked over to Jen for her approval. She nodded and we went crazy, grabbing almost everything off the racks.

I tried on about seven dresses that I loved, three pairs

of jeans, five blouses that were undeniably cute, and four suits that screamed *promotion*. I skipped out of the dressing room with my arms full of clothes. Jen and I walked to the checkout counter and plopped our things on the counter.

"Alright! Looks like someone is treating herself today!" said the clerk.

"I sure am!"

"So how long has this shop been here?" asked Jen.

"Well it's fairly new, I just got the space."

"Wait, this is your line?" I asked.

"It sure is! I'm Natasha Sample, designer and owner of NES Fashions."

"Man, you are amazing! I am very busty, and these tops fit perfectly!" said Jen.

"Why, thank you. I see you picked some of my favorites. What shoes are you wearing with this dress?" She held up the lightly dimmed, soft pink cocktail dress. I stared at it and tried to remember what I had in my closet. The images I came up with in my head were my three-inch work heels, my flats, and my sneakers.

"I have no idea. Jen, let's go to the shoe section in Nordstrom and see what they have."

"Great idea, they have some Steve Maddens that will look good with your choices," said Natasha.

Before Natasha rang us up, we chatted a little longer and she handed me her card. She said most of her stuff would be online at www.nesfashions.com. (Check it out; the site is awesome. No, seriously. Stop reading and check it out; this is a real site.)

Jen and I walked back to the Nordstrom shoe section and started to sort through the Betsy Johnson, Jessica Simpson, and Steve Madden shoes. Jen walked over to the wall and basically had a mini orgasm in the middle of the floor. She picked up a pair of Jessica Simpson heels—beige with a red heel and gold sole; seemed I wasn't the only one in need of a treat today. We walked out of there with about five pairs of shoes, ringing my total up to $575.26. My wallet was screaming, *Mommy, stop*! I ignored the pain and swiped my card anyway.

"Alright, so you have a GREAT selection of clothes!"

"Yes, I do."

"But there is now one last thing we must do!"

"And what is that?"

"Your hair."

"Oh, no, Jen, I love my hair!"

"Yeah, and apparently shampoo doesn't. So come on, let's go."

She dragged me across the hall to a high-profile salon

called Sweetness. This salon stays busy, and you usually have to make appointments four weeks in advance. But apparently Jen had connections. One of her clients at the gym was the owner and master stylist, who owed Jen a huge favor. We walked up to the desk to a very hot Hispanic lady with dark hair, nice boobs, red lips, and eyes that would pierce through your skull.

"Ay, tank you for calling Sweetness, how can we make you sweet?" she said as she answered the phone. "Umm, huh, okay. I see. Well he is busy, I will take a message and have him call you back." She hung up the phone and stared at us while chewing her gum.

"Hey. I'm Jen, and we have an appointment with Bernard." Everyone gasped and stared. Soon the whole salon was looking at us like we'd said we had a nuclear bomb in our purses.

"Very good, follow me." She got up in her skintight pencil skirt paired up with a red blouse and black Louboutins. "He's right this way." She directed us to the exclusive part of the salon in the far right-hand corner. She gave two knocks on the door then left. Soon the door swung open; there was this bright-ass light that came through, along with a breeze. Soon I saw someone walking—I wanted to say Jesus? But I figured that this was Bernard.

"Jen-Jen! Oooh, come here, my love!" He extended his arms as he walked with purpose towards Jen.

"S'up, Bernard! Here is my friend Hope."   They broke hold and he stared at me, screamed a little, and stared some more.

"*Ay, Dios mío*! Look at dis hair! I need baby Jesus for you, honey."

"Well, pull out the Bible and get to work," said Jen. I gave her a glare, and she assured me I was in capable hands.

"So how long, Bernard?"

"Give me about two hours."

"Sounds good! Hey, Hope, have fun, I'm gonna go watch *Twilight*."

There I was, all alone with Bernard, who kept speaking Spanish. I guess he wasn't happy with my hair. He walked me over to the sink and made sure I had a rough cleaning and deep conditioning. As I sat under the dryer with my mayonnaise mask on my head, I was looking through some styles I might want to try. I showed him my choices and he loved them all, but we agreed on one particular style. Soon it was time to rinse, and the cutting began. Two hours seemed to go by hella fast. Now I saw why women liked going to the salon; I found out about all the new gossip and drama in all of Arizona.

I was in such awe with this whole being a cute female thing I didn't even notice that my phone was dinging. I'd gotten a message from Richie.

Hey you, hope you're having a great day what are your plans later? I was hoping you'd want to go to dinner with me?

I smiled and screamed; people were looking at me like I was insane. Then I explained that this awesome guy finally had asked me out! I said yes, of course, and he insisted that we meet around eight at a great sushi bar called Mr. Tim's. I looked at my watch and saw that it was already seven thirty p.m.; I had about fifteen minutes left to style (at least that's what Bernard said), but what was I going to wear?

"Bernard, so I said yes."

"Sí?!"

"YES! To Richie! Now what do I wear?"

"Well, honey, you just went shopping."

"You are right!"

"Now, would you like a little makeup added at no cost?"

"Sure!"

"María! Come here! Our frog-turned-princess has a date in thirty minutes, let's work our magic!"

María then skipped over with her trusty makeup kit.

She looked at my skin and smiled. She said my skin was amazing, and then she went to work. I felt like I had the superstar treatment: my hair being done by one of the best stylists in Arizona, my makeup done by María, and wearing a dress by NES Fashions and shoes from Steve Madden.

"Hey, Bernard! It's been two hours, how does she look?!" Jen said as she skipped into the salon, happier than normal.

"Well, mi amor, look for yourself!"

He spun me around and Jen's jaw dropped. She was looking at her new BFF. I'd changed my hair to a chocolate brown, my makeup was minimal but did enough to make me gorgeous, and my outfit was sexy. Jen pretty much cry-hugged me and spun me around.

"Oh, my baby! You look amazing! Mama is proud!"

"Thanks! Richie just texted me and I'm meeting him across the street at Mr. Tim's for dinner."

"WHAT! When?!"

"Like now."

"Well go get him, tiger! Don't worry about your stuff, I'll put it in the car. And Hope, please take my peacoat, that damn North Face is a wreck."

"Thanks, Jen."

I smiled, hugged Bernard and María, said bye to the

salon, and made my way to Mr. Tim's.

So Proud of Hope

Jen did exactly as she said she would do. She grabbed the bags, waddled to the car, and threw them into the trunk. Unlocking the driver's door, she jumped into the seat and turned on the radio. She started to head out of the garage when something strange jumped in the way. Jen slammed on her breaks and skidded down the ramp until she saw a light. First she thought it was baby Jesus paying her a visit, but it was just the exit. She then jumped out of the car and looked up, trying to see if something was on the ramp. Soon someone came down the ramp extremely fast. She squinted and tried to get focus, but the blur was too fast. She then got ran over by some tween on a skateboard.

"Hey, sorry, lady," said the kid.

"What the hell is wrong with you?!"

"Well you should learn how to drive."

"Or MAYBE you shouldn't be skateboarding in a parking garage, you idiot!"

"Fair enough," he said as he picked up his skateboard. "So I won't sue you for ruining my wheel. I'll let this one go, since you're a total MILF."

"A MILF?"

"Yeah, you know, a mother I'd like to f—"

"Yeah, I know! I'm not a mom."

"Well you're still hot. Can I get your number?"

"HA! In your dreams! I can still smell the Enfamil on your breath, young one."

"Whatever, octo-mom"

"Beat it, Justin Bieber."

As Jen refrained from smacking the living daylights out of that kid, she hopped in the car and proceeded to head home. Right when she reached the driveway, Jen wasn't so happy with what she saw. It was a Chevy truck, right smack dab in the middle, parked as crooked as ever. She then parked her car by the mailbox and dragged all the clothes and shoes inside by herself. Opening the door, she saw Sean and Ray on the couch, playing Xbox.

"Hey, Jen!" they said in unison.

"Seriously, how do you guys get in here?"

"We have our ways," said Sean as he sipped on his slushie.

"Like how? You don't have a key."

"Well, little Barbie, we have our ways," said Ray as he lifted his eyebrow.

"Whatever, freak faces. So ya'll should help me with this crap."

"What is that?" asked Sean.

"All Hope's crap."

"Well where is Hope?" asked Ray.

"On a date."

"WHAT!" they said.

"Yeah, Richie texted her while she was in the middle of getting sexy."

"And our sweet Hope said yes?"

"Yup!"

"Aww," Ray said, "I may cry."

"Well don't, thick skull; it's not a pretty sight."

"Well, asses, thanks for NOT helping me with this crap. Anyways she will be home soon, they just went to sushi."

"Ooh la la, he plans on getting some," said Sean.

"Why would you say that?" asked Ray.

"Cuz sushi releases this sex hormone in the ladies, making them all horny and stuff."

"Is that why you bring me sushi almost every day?" asked Jen.

"Yes, and for the fact that it's on my way here." Sean smiled.

"Okay, Sean buddy, you're wrong," said Ray.

"What are you talking about, sushi makes the chicks

horny."

"Um, no, Sean, that would be oysters."

"Yeah, isn't that some form of sushi?"

"No," Jen snapped.

"Oh, so if I get you oysters, then you'd get all hot and want to jump this?"

"One..."

"Ray, what is she doing?"

"Two..."

"Oh, she's counting."

"Three..."

"For why?"

"Four..."

"Because when she gets to five, she's going to attack you, preferably your face."

"What?!"

"FIVE!"

Like clockwork, Jen managed to jump over the counter and chase Sean all throughout the house. As Sean kept screaming for help from Ray, Ray just sat back and watched this unfold.

"Dude, I keep telling you leave them white girls alone, they will kill you and you'll be on *Snapped*!"

"But you're around white chicks all the time!"

"Yes, and I also hook them up and have to get to know them, wicked species they are."

"DAMN IT, JEN! Stop biting! Ray, HELP!"

"No sir, buddy. Jen has man-monkey strength. Can't help ya on this. Oh, and Jen, try not to make him bleed this time.

Mr. Tim's

As I walked into Mr. Tim's, my hands were sweating and I started to panic a little. Everyone in there was smiling, happy, and all cuddly towards each other. Even the hostess seemed like she was high. She offered to seat me, but I refused because a trip to the bathroom was very much needed. I walked as fast as I could while still trying to look sexy. I reached the bathroom door and basically threw myself in. I stared at myself in the mirror, trying to give myself a pep talk. I paced back and forth, pumping myself up like I was in the Super Bowl. I even did an invisible chest bump and butt slap to myself. As people walked into the bathroom, they walked out just as fast. Did I notice? Yes, but did I care? Not at all. I finally calmed down, wiped off my sweat and running makeup, smiled in the mirror, and headed out the door.

115

"Good evening, ma'am," said the adorable hostess.

"Hello."

"Would you like to sit?"

"No, thank you, I will wait in the bar."

She acknowledged me and directed me towards the bar area. I sat there in my sexy dress and some six inch stilettos (that I could barely walk in), hair and makeup done, and ordered my Jack and Coke. I watched a little TV and even talked with the bartender for a few minutes. As I was laughing and enjoying being the center of attention, my phone buzzed. I looked down and it was a text from Richie.

"You look astonishing tonight, seems like that bartender is

into you ;) "

I giggled a little and turned around in my chair. There he was, all six feet, three inches with a natural tan, bright eyes, and a Crest smile. We stared at each other for about 10 seconds before either of us said anything.

"Hey. Richie?"

"Hello, doll, these are for you."

He gave me a kiss on the cheek while handing me some flowers. They weren't roses; instead they were lilies wrapped in baby's breath.

"Would you like to have a seat?"

I nodded and walked towards the restaurant.

"Wahoo, tiger, where you going?"

"Well, towards the restaurant, silly, that's where people eat."

"True. But tonight you and I will be sitting somewhere else."

He then took my hand and directed me towards the back through the kitchen to an elevator. He pressed the button and we waited until the doors opened. After what seemed like forever, the doors finally opened and he directed me into the elevator, which was nicely decorated with lace and flowers.

"Do restaurant elevators always look this fancy?"

"Only because you are here," he responded.

He looked into my eyes and kissed my forehead. Standing behind me with his arms draped over my shoulders, he pushed the button to the roof. I closed my eyes. As my heart started to beat faster, I could feel his heart beat just as fast against my back. Soon the doors opened and we were at the top of the building. He grabbed my hand and walked me out the elevator towards the middle of the rooftop.

From where we left the elevator to where the table was, the path was lined with blue rose petals, and there were lights draped along the poles, which happened to be decorated in lace. Then the table sat in the middle of the roof with a guy waiting to pull out our chairs. I sat down and looked around in amazement. The time and effort was well thought out.

"So, I don't do this a lot," said Richie.

"What do you mean? Dropping money on women?"

"No, I do that only for those who are worth it. Tonight I got excited. I really wanted to make this first date and meeting something special."

"Well, you really succeeded. As long as there is no one coming out playing the violin, then we will be fine."

"Why? You don't like classical music?"

"No, I hate classical music, but I don't want this to seem too cliché, like we are in a movie or something."

"I see you are not the typical lady. Which is why I didn't spring for the violin." He laughed a little while sipping on his champagne.

"So how did you get all this? I mean do you know the owner?"

"Yes, I do actually. A really good guy."

"Wow, really? How did you two meet?"

"Well, I see him on a daily basis."

"Connections must be nice," I said as I sipped from my glass.

"Yeah, I do love myself and my accomplishments."

Sitting there stunned and not knowing what to say, I stared at Richie for a while, trying to read in his eyes if he was telling the truth or not.

"So you're Mr. Tim?"

"Well, yes and no. I bought the restaurant from a man I met in India. I go there a lot to help the kids and the country. He owned this place, and when it was going under, I bought him out."

"Wow, so did he need to be bought out?"

"Yes and no. Yes because he was dying of cancer and had no immediate children to leave it to, and no because he's well off and had tons of people trying to buy this spot."

"So why settle on you?"

"Because I helped his wife and his nephews. I proved I'm trustworthy. One time I went to see him, and his nephew was playing in the river. A car came speeding through the projects and hit his nephew. He got ran over, and if I wasn't there to apply pressure to the wound and take them to the hospital, he would've died."

"Wow, that is amazing."

"Enough about me, Hope, tell me about you."

"Well I work for Sharps, Inc., and I'm the top executive there and assistant to the boss."

"I read up on them. Your boss's name is Kelly?"

119

"Yes how did you know?"

"We were in business once. She is a mess and a little bit of a tool."

"Hey, you said it, not me. And besides that, I just have a great group of friends and family."

"Any hobbies?"

"No, not really. Just a plain Jane who goes with the flow."

"Well nothing wrong with that, Jane. Maybe I can be your Tarzan and open your eyes a little."

"I would like that."

We got into a deep conversation about sports—the new rules with the NFL and the NBA lockout. Then our conversation switched to family, friends, work, and the basic questions when getting to know someone. Soon our food arrived and our plates were just as gorgeous as the décor. We ate, laughed, smiled, and hugged until it was time for us to leave.

"Well, Cinderella, it's midnight and we should get you home."

"Okay, thank you for such a great night."

"Thank you for saying yes on such a short notice."

We waited outside the restaurant until the valet pulled

his car around. He opened my door to his 2015 Audi, ran to his side, and took me home. Once we reached my house, he opened my door again and walked me to the door.

* * *

Dear Diary,

So I may actually think he is the one. I know it's only been one date, but when you know, you know, right? Well fingers crossed.

<3 Becoming a Romantic Hope

Hope Loves Sleep!

"Is she up?"

"IDK, Ray, why don't you knock?!" snapped Jen.

"Did you just IDK me?"

"Yes, I D.I.D!"

"Shut up, we are not on the computer, dipdong."

Ray and Jen crept into my room, staring at me while I slept. Soon to follow was our lovely friend Sean.

"Hey!"

"SHHH!" Ray and Jen said.

"The door was open so I thought I'd come in."

"Man, shut up! What part of SHHH do you not understand?" said Ray.

"Umm, shh because I don't subject myself to doing

what others want. It's so robotic."

"Okay, redonk face!" said Jen. "Just shut your hole!"

"Shut my hole? It's easy for me to do, what about you?" Sean said as his eyes glanced down at Jen's private parts.

"Ooh, you're an ass!" Jen then lunged at Sean, and sha-boom, they fell right on me.

"DAMN IT, GUYS! It's bad enough NONE of you can whisper, now I have slushie on my face and hairspray residue in my eye. THANKS!"

"Aw, you're such a doll in the morning!" said Ray.

Throwing bleach blond and dip doe to the ground, I got up and headed towards the bathroom. Why were these weirdos following me?

"Sooo, tell us about him!" said Ray.

"Yeah, you bang him?" asked Jen.

"How's his motherboard?" asked Sean.

" BTDubs you all are freaks." I walked into the bathroom, shutting the door to take a nice hot shower. I turned the shower on, waited for the water to get hot, and then slipped right in. I grabbed my shampoo and conditioner and started to sing my lungs out to Bruno Mars's song "Grenade." Right when I was at my peak, the high point, about to hit the best note ever, the three stooges stormed right on in.

"WTF?!! Ugh! Are you guys serious?!" I screamed.

"Um, yes we are, Athena," said Sean as he slurped on his gigantic Slurpee.

"Soo, tell us about him! Did you meet him on my site?" asked Ray.

"God, if you did meet Mr. Tim on his site, that is a definite no-no, and he gots to go."

"Oh, hush up, Barbie!"

Soon Ray and Jen were exchanging plenty of words, a majority of which didn't make sense at all.

"Okay! STOP! He is awesome, we ate, we kissed, we talked, and we have another date!"

"See, Hope, now was that so hard?" asked Sean. "We only wanted to be the nosiest bunch of brats you love and are used to."

"Whatevs, Sean. So since I told you, why don't ya'll go somewhere else besides my bathroom."

"So is this the fellow you met from Bang then?" asked Ray.

"Well, duh! She has no life, so therefore there is no chance she can meet him anywhere else."

"Thanks, Jen."

"Hey, Ms. Anti Social, don't be mean to Jen. She's

right, you are a lame. If it wasn't for me in your life then you would prob still be bored and, well, lame," said Sean as he sipped on that damn slushie.

"Okay, I thought that fell on the floor," I said.

"Well it did."

"So how is there still crap in it?"

"Because I scooped it back in there."

We all stopped and looked at Sean. Knowing he was telling the truth just made me want to throw up.

"Okay…Mr. Dirt Slurper, salior-mouth Barbie, and wannabe romantic guru, get out."

They all looked at each other and smiled, gave me huge, unwelcome kisses on my face, then walked out one by one.

After being harassed and complaining to my bestest friend (my diary), I finally had to head to work. I drove my little beater to my job and putt-putted my way into a parking spot. Slamming my door, I made my way to the elevator (because the stairs would've probably kicked my ass), dragging myself, moaning and groaning, and mean-mugging everyone who said hi to me. Okay, I must admit, I did look like death, but hey, I was interrupted. I looked like a mix of Medusa and Michael Jackson, but I thought I still looked hot. The door hadn't closed yet and I couldn't tell if people wanted to stay on or run for their lives.

"Floor four, please," I asked the skinny Asian man who was standing by the buttons, pressing the door open button. He kept looking at me and slowly raised his hand to touch my hair.

"Does it hurt?" he asked.

"What hurt?"

"Being hit by lightening?"

I stared at him, not sure if he was joking or not. When his face didn't move, I realized he was serious. I walked out, turned around to the crowded elevator, and said, "No, it didn't hurt. When you're Satan's spawn you can handle pain!" I growled and walked away laughing. I still remember the look on that uptight lady's face who probably was praying, and if she'd had holy water I would've been saved.

Still laughing all the way towards my desk, I plopped down in my seat, kicked my feet up, and leaned back. After about five minutes of shuteye time, I opened my eyes to see Kelly's perky boobs on my cubical walls.

"What?" I said.

"Soo, looks like someone has an admirer!"

"What are you speaking of, boss lady."

"Boss lady, I like that! Well your roses, silly!" she said as she jumped up and skipped away. I turned my chair around and saw a huge bouquet of roses. Red ones, white ones, and pink ones, all in one precious bouquet in a glass vase with a bow around it. I looked all around, blushing and trying not to pee myself. I smelled them over and over. Getting lost in the sweet scent of my flowers, I cut my nose on the card. Grabbing my little nose I snatched the card and read the inscription.

To my lovely Hope,
I hope I get to on Friday.
You pick the spot,
I'll pick you up at 7.
-Your Mr. Right
aka it's me, Richie ☺

I put the card down and sat in my lame chair. I was spinning around with butterflies and high hopes when my chair stopped spinning. I got even more pissy that someone would ruin my fairytale, only-happens-in-movies moment. Soon my smile turned into a scowl.

"KELLY! What do you want, for the love of all things that aren't plastic, what do you want?" She stood there, reading my card and giggling. "What is so funny?"

"This dude is in love with you, poor thing." As she tossed my card to the side, she said, "Too bad you can't go."

"Why wouldn't I be able to go?"

"Because you and I have a very important dinner with a big executive company."

"And I'm going and not the brunette version of you because…?"

"Well because I need your brains. I have the looks and charm, now I just need someone to deliver a banging business proposal. If we land this, then Sharps will have a multi-billion-dollar partner. So what do you say? Should we do Tim's at seven?"

I sat there in my chair, happy but mad. Happy because I was coming along on the biggest deal to ever come to Sharps, which could only mean one thing: I was up for a promotion! But then I was mad because my prince charming wanted to wine and dine me again. Man, I knew I should've thought about it first before saying yes., Now I forgot and I'm in a pickle, cancel my date or my meeting?

"Okay, so you're taking, like, FOREVER to answer me! How about this, bring along Mr. Right."

"Really?"

"Yes."

"Why?"

"Well, these hot shots are all men, if we bring along a male who appears to be strong, confident, and honest, they may think the same of us. Plus it's in two days so you have time to prep him."

"But Richie doesn't work here."

"Duh, I know, silly! But they don't know that. We just need him to dress to impress, nod when we speak, and look intelligent. He's perfectly capable of being eye candy, right? I mean, this guy is cute?"

"Well, I'll ask him."

"Thanks! Toodles!"

The mere thought of being around Kelly when this moment was supposed to be intimate brought on thoughts of me ending up on an episode of *Snapped*. But hey, big bucks were in the near future. I hoped Richie was on board.

Sitting at my desk thinking about how I could ask Richie to join us for dinner seemed to be the hardest thing I would ever have to do. I mean, come on! We'd only been out once. Yes, I was totally smitten, and duh, this guy made me weak with just one look, WHICH was why he couldn't come to this meeting! Didn't this scream, *Hey, I'm a clingy douche and I need you around me 24/7*? Ugh, I know it screamed that, so stop saying no and smiling. As I laid my head on my desk, slowly banging it on the keyboard, my cellular device rang.

I slowly looked up, searching for my phone with a Post-it note stuck to my head. I dumped my purse open, then my desk drawers, and couldn't find this phone anywhere! Soon, as it was on its last ring, I remembered it was in my boobs. Looking down to a missed call from Richie, I quickly hit the call back button.

"Hey, you! I thought I drove you away," said Richie as I continued, with an awkward laugh and snort, to pull myself together and try to help finish the conversation.

"Hey, sun drop!"

Sun drop? What the hell, Hope! "So what's cookin', good lookin'?" *Oh, sweet baby Jesus, what am I saying?*

"Sun drop, huh? I like that! Well I just wanted to call and wish you a happy day at work. I also wanted to know if you got my flowers and if you wanted to go out on Friday?"

Okay, Hope, you got this. Stop smiling over the phone and get your balls together and ask him!

"Oh, yeah, those awesome flowers! Of course I got them, they are awesome!"

"Great! Soooo..."

"Oh, yes, as for friday, I would love to go to dinner but..."

As I finally got the balls to ask him to come hang at din-din, guess who was listening and grabbed my phone. That's right: Kelly!

"Hey, is this hot face?"

"Ummmm, yes?" said Richie.

"Sweet. So check this, okay, Ms. Lonely Vag would love to eat with your sexy mouth again in hopes of landing that—aka you—in the sack. BUT here's the thing, cat eyes, she has a very important business dinner tonight including me—her boss, of course—and a big, billion-dollar company. SOOO Ms. Lonely Pants can't go with you. Unless you wouldn't mind joining along, being our eye candy, and helping us seal the deal, and then you can finally seal her deal. So what do you say?"

"Ahhhhh...sure?"

"Great! Here's your lady." Handing me the phone, she skipped away while flipping her hair. I couldn't help but feel the awkward silence between us and that made my heart drop.

"Hey, hello?" he asked.

"Oh, hey! Yeah, that was, umm…"

"Kelly? Your boss?"

"Yeah."

"What a character, huh?! Well, since I'll be joining

you, I can't wear a suit I've already worn then, huh?"

"I guess not!" I said as I began to smile big.

"And since I'm getting a new suit, you need a new dress too, then?"

"Possibly, seeing how the only dress I own was the one I wore last night."

"Hmm, this sounds like an emergency! Three-way me into your boss's office."

Shocked by his reply, I reluctantly did what he asked.

"Hey, Kelly?"

"What's up?! Finally want to tell me you want to be friends and mimic my existence?"

"Umm, no, Richie wants to tell you something?"

"Okay? Shoot, sexy mouth."

"Okay, so Hope is going to need the day off." My eyes got really big and I lost my breath. "Mainly because if we are going to nail this proposal, we need to brainstorm all day! You know, like power thinking?"

"Wow, you are so smart!" Kelly said, then her thin neck whipped towards me. "Hey, cobweb cotter, you can go home. See you at Tim's on Friday, seven p.m. Don't be late or early!"

Not knowing what the hell that meant, I did as she said, closed her door, and spun around with excitement. "So why do I need the day off? You know I'm not brainstorming all day, right?"

"Of course not! We are going shopping!"

"Really?!"

"Yes! And it's on me. Seeing how I can't have you alone for dinner on Friday, I'll take up your afternoon and possibly evening. I'll pick you up at your house in thirty minutes."

After hanging up the phone, I was super excited to go on about my day. Kelly left her office door open and her phone began to ring.

"Hello?" Kelly said as she stared out her window. "So this is perfect. Get her alone more, talk to her, get in her head. I need her little brain and then I can let her ass go. You are the key in this distraction. We must stick together on this!" As the conversation went quiet, I crept up on her door, trying to listen in on what Kelly was talking about. "Ricky, I don't care! As family we call on favors, remember! Operation Plan Hope is in full effect!"

"Knock, knock!" I said as I entered her office.

"Shoot, gotta go! Hey, Hope, what's up?"

"Just letting you know that I'm leaving."

"Okay, goodbye! See you later!"

Operation Plan Hope. Why does that sound familiar?

Seems like I've heard that before; I just don't know where or when.

Got in my car and texted Richie that I was on the way home. He promptly responded with "*I'll beat you there;)*" . Oh how he was so cute! I rushed to get home only to look in my review mirror to see him pulling up right behind me.

"Hey there gorgeous!"

"Hey you!" he held me tight and gave me a nice kiss

"Ready to go shopping?"

"That is one question you never have to ask a lady!" He opened the car door for me as I slid into the passenger seat nice and comfy. My phone kept buzzing. It was Jen wanting to know about you BFF night in that we planned awhile ago. I'll text her later.

"Ready to rock n roll doll?"

"Yes I am! Let's go!"

After a full day of shopping, frozen yogurt and we managed to sneak in a movie, I was beat! Now when I say a full day we were in and out of the mall. I'm a fast shopper, I hate the slow walk around and looking at every piece of clothing in the store. I like to look and if nothing peaks my interest than I keep it moving. Richie doesn't complain because honestly what guy likes to shop for a long time?

Before we knew it, it was 5pm and we were in my driveway.

"Ugh! I dont want to say bye" I complained as I unbuckled my seat belt

"Well don't"

"Meaning?"

"Meaning, I go home-shower- come back and pick you up for dinner?"

"Deal, see you in a couple hours"

"Eight, be ready by eight"

Right when I got to my room and threw my bags on the floor I received a message from Jen. She said she's so excited to hangout tonight. How could I forget! We planned this BFF night IN like two months ago! I think I even have it circled, stared, and highlighted out all up on my calendar. What should I do? Well the sensible person would text back hoping that she would understand that I have a BIG date, or maybe I should lie and say a meeting? But this is me we are talking about so instead I'll just ignore her message... again.

A couple hours passed by and I was almost ready. I was nervous, sweating, shaking and I wanted to throw up! NO scratch that I NEEDED to throw up! I kept hearing some strange noises so I turned my music down and heard Jen coming in. Shoot! I forgot to text her back canceling this BFF night in. Okay, let's play it cool Hope. Slowly turn the music back up, turn off my phone I'll act as if it was off for a majority of the day, and when she asks, I'll have an easy alibi. Man I do lobe talking to myself; I give the best advice!

Walking to her room I could hear Jen throw her purse down. She knocked on the bathroom door all happy until she saw me dressed to kill.

"So where are you headed?"

"Oh just have a meeting to attend"

"What about BFF night in?"

"Sorry soul sista, we will have to reschedule"

" I text you"

"did you? Oh man my phone is off I'm sorry"

"Yeah well it wasn't off when I texted"

"How would you know?"

"Because you have read receipt on your phone aka it tells me when you read my messages. Nice try to ditch me. All you had to say was that you did want to go. Lying just takes away major points"

"Well I'm glad we aren't playing jeopardy"

Jen looked at me in disgust and disappointment as I struggled to make a wedged eyeliner. I could tell she was sad but I had no time to tend to her feelings. Am I wrong?

"Jen I'm sorry just a little agitated. How about we

135

reschedule for tomorrow night?"

"Just you and me?"

"Of course!"

"Okay, deal"

Yeah I know I have that meeting tomorrow night with the company and Richie, but I will just act as if something new came about. No biggie... right?

Dear Diary,

Dinner was amazing! I felt like poo for lying to my boo. I couldn't tell her that I would rather go on a date than to hear her complain about her love life. I mean mine is going great so I have to stay positive right? Keep the good vibes around? Well I have a lot to think about until next time

Feeling a little off - Hope

Okay, Let's Seal This Deal

All day I've been a nervous wreck! I usually would talk to Jen but I've been ignoring her messages. I finally told her I couldn't make BFF night in AGAIN and she didn't text me back. Crappy day, lead to getting yelled at while at work, now leads to an awkward dinner after an even more awkward confrontation with Jen.

"You is kind, you is smart, you is important!" I said to myself as I looked into the mirror. After applying my makeup and pushing up my boobs, my dress was as sexy as ever!

"So tonight. The big meeting with Mr. Sexy, huh?" asked Jen as she chomped on some Pops cereal.

"Yes."

"Are you ready? You sure you don't need to jack anymore lines from *The Help* to put some more fire under your ass?"

"Oh, shut your face! Just because you can't recite inspirational lines doesn't mean I can't!"

"Umm, you got me on that one! Because I bet you can really relate to what those women went through—"

"Oh, can it, Barbie!"

"Ouch! Looks like my little peanut still has fight and didn't fully change into a dipshit like I thought."

Glaring at me through the mirror, Jen left the bathroom door to finish her cereal. The doorbell shortly rang, and then soon after, a knock.

"Hey, uptighty whitey, your date is at the door!" yelled Jen.

"Can you get it?"

"Yeah I could, but I'm too busy watching *The Help* so I can be as educated and get really thoughtful, resourceful lines that I can use at random moments in my life!"

"You're such a dick!"

"At least I can get some!"

I stomped to the door and slammed it shut. Tonight I'd planned to introduce Jen to Richie, but she was a fire pistol right now, and that wouldn't be good. Maybe next time.

"Hey, gorgeous! You look great!"

"Thank you! You don't look bad yourself."

"Are you ready to tackle this meeting?"

"Hells yeah, I am!"

We got into his car and drove to Tim's, brainstorming in the car about what to say and when he should nod. I was just giving him a little insight, just in case they were to ask him some questions, so he wouldn't be totally oblivious.

We pulled up to Tim's right at seven p.m., like Kelly said, not early and not late. I took a huge breath in and out, rolled my neck and cracked my knuckles, jumped out of the car and smacked Richie on the butt, and headed in. Okay, I did all that except for jump out of the car and smack tight ass on the rear. Sounded good, though.

"Hope! So if we seal this deal, that new VP spot could be yours," said a very calm and surprisingly covered-up Kelly.

"Wow!"

"Okay, we are at that table. Bring the boy toy."

"No problem," I said, looking back at Richie, nudging him to come on. As we headed in that direction, I felt a slight tug on my arm.

"Richie, what's up?"

"I'm nerves! What if I blow the game, coach? What if I get pulled off the bench and freeze?! Oh my gosh, what if I fart and—"

Giving him a quick smack to the face, I got Richie back to normal.

"HEY! You can do this, champ!! If you get pulled off the bench, you own that field! This is our game and we will win this shit!"

Nothing like a great pep talk to get the night started. Getting our composure together, we sat at the table, where Kelly introduced us to the big shot billionaires.

"This is Hope, or VP of Sharps, and this is Mr. Toka, the CEO, Mrs. Simo, the COO, and Mr. Husa, the treasurer of Yotaki, Inc."

"VP of Sharps?" I whispered.

"You could be, now shush."

"And this is Richard. He is our correspondent."

Richie bowed to Yotaki, Inc., and they responded with a bow. We all sat at the table, starting off with small talk, like their flight and how they liked Arizona so far.

"So, Mr. Toka, why do you want to merge with Sharps?" asked Kelly.

"Well, merging is the new 'it' thing to do. Merging with a great American company can bring many treasures and income, if done properly."

"Mrs. Simo, do you have any concerns?" I asked.

"Yes, mine would be how well you can keep up your end of the bargain. Unfortunately for you, we merged with an American business before and we got stood up and lots of profit was lost."

Great, they had been burned before and we were the hush puppies, the experiment, and there was a great chance that we wouldn't seal this deal. Kelly and I looked at each other because we knew we had to bring up our A-game to land them.

"We understand that, but here at Sharps we keep true to our word and our appearance."

"Funny you should say 'appearance,' because your president, Ms. Kelly, has been in the headlines, and not in good ways. A partier, surgery-addictive woman is what the last newsletter said," implied Mr. Husa.

This was when shit got real. They'd already done their research. They probably knew more about Sharps, Inc. than the two of us combined.

"Well, sir, product placement and attention," Richie said.

We all stared in his direction, and I was praying that this would end well.

"Excuse me?" Mr. Husa said.

"Product placement and attention. It's no surprise that Sharps and Yotaki have been down in the dumps and sales for both parties haven't been going well. But whenever Kelly is in the newsletter and word gets out about her antics, have you noticed the rise in sales?"

"Well I never looked at that before," Mrs. Simo said.

"Take this for instance. Madonna, before an album or

perfume drops, she stirs up some type of confusion. Why? To draw the attention back to her. Then, when she's in the middle, she drops that album or fragrance, and BOOM, sales go up. Think of Kelly as the Madonna of Sharps."

Richie stopped talking to let Yotaki, Inc. think. He sat back so smoothly and drank his beer with a smirk on his face. He glanced at me and winked, then looked at Kelly and nodded. From then on, the table talked all night, ate dinner, and had a few drinks. Laughter and knowledge surrounded our table. After a good two and a half hours of wining and dining our guests, they finally decided to seal the deal. That's right, thanks to my pep talk to Richie, the covered-up dress worn by Kelly, and my brains, we knocked the deal out of the ball park!

On the way home, Richie said he wanted to make a detour. We drove to the top of the world and we looked down at all of Tucson. Nothing screamed *romance* like being in the middle of nowhere, watching the lights, and hearing random animal noises.

"Hey, Richie, want to come over tomorrow night? Watch a movie or something?"

"I would love to, but I can't. I have to work late tomorrow. But later this week I'm all yours."

I smiled and agreed to the arrangements. Soon

enough he was walking me to my door, giving me a kiss on the lips and also on the forehead.

* * *

Dear Diary,

I love being jumped early in the morning as I try to make myself pretty and loveable for work. But why must having the most redonk friends come with the territory? Maybe I was some kind of witch, heathen, or even serial killer in my former life. Yeah, that HAS to be it. Baby Jesus is punishing me, and I have no idea why. By the way, we sealed the deal! Big thanks to Richie, and I believe I'm in love! No, I don't think we are going too fast, but of course I will always pay attention and keep a slight guard up. Goodnight. <3
Hope

Girl Hang Time?

Waking up the next morning to a loud Jen screaming lyrics to random songs, I realized I'd had the most peaceful night's sleep that I'd ever had. Walking into the bathroom, I saw my hairspray was missing because someone was using it as a microphone, so I made my way into the living room to battle the diva so I could finish getting ready.

"Hey, Jen!"

"HIT ME WITH YOUR BEST SHOT!"

"Jen?!"

"FIRE

AWAAAAAAAAAAAAAAAAAAAAAAAAAA—"

"YO, PAT BENATAR!"

"Oh! WHAT UP?!"

"Can I have my hairspray?"

"OH, DUDE! No way, I was just about to do some sick air guitar!"

"Figured you would say that, sooo, instead here is the blow dryer. You can use the chord."

"Awesome!"

"So you wanna hang tonight?!"

"Nope."

"Ugh, why not?"

"Because this hot mama has a date!"

"Really? Jen, that's great, with who?!"

"This guy I met on Bang, he is awesome! He's super busy and successful, lives in Phoenix, and he's in town tonight and is meeting me for dinner!"

"AWESOME! Where to?"

"Where else? Tim's! He supposedly has the hookup there."

"Look at you, all girly and shit! I love it! Well, if you

don't scare him away I wanna meet this guy sometime!"

"How was your date with Richie last night?"

"GOOD! He's busy tonight so I'll just fire up the ol' DVD player myself and relax."

"Cool! Well, have a great day at work. My first client isn't until three this afternoon so I'm hanging out."

As I walked out the door, hairspray in hand, I was super happy for Jen! This meant we could double date, maybe have a double wedding and so on! Okay, I knew I was getting ahead of myself, but I would've loved it if this happened.

Kelly, my New BFF?

I was having a great morning! My BFF had a new beau, my new beau was totally infatuated with me and vice versa, and I'd just helped my boss land our biggest client/partner. Even though my car stopped on me four times as I was driving to work, I didn't mind at all. I was oblivious to the massive amount of bird shit that was on my car, didn't even notice the huge crack in my windshield, and apparently I didn't notice my surprise in the back seat, either.

As I stopped the car, I looked down to unbuckle my seatbelt and grabbed my purse that was chilling in the passenger seat. I flipped down my mirror and checked my hair and makeup. Turning around to see if I'd forgot about anything, I smacked faces with Sean.

"What the hell?!"

"Hey, Athena!"

"UGH, SEAN! What do you want?!"

"Remember today you were giving me a ride to work? This is not my work, this is your job."

"DAMN IT! Why didn't you say anything?!"

"How could I?! You were in complete murder mode of singing "Little Red Corvette" by Prince. I didn't want to miss the concert. Oh, and by the way, you didn't hit that one note in the second ver—"

"SEAN! Okay, now I'm at work, I can't take you to work. So what are you going to do?" As he sipped his slushie he seemed to be thinking pretty hard.

"Hmm, no worries, I'll think of something."

I started to get out of my car and noticed Sean wasn't moving. "Yo, you getting out? I gotta lock my doors." Sean busted out in a high-pitched laugh.

"Athena, its coo', not like someone is going to steal this beauty."

"Whatever! Lock the doors when you're done." As I walked away I heard a car start. Reaching the front of my building, I looked back to check on Sean and my car; I was beginning to feel bad about forgetting. Then there Sean was, in my car, driving away. Man I really needed to get a new car because if my car started without the keys, then that definitely wasn't good.

Still not letting being carjacked by one of my friends ruin my day, I headed into work to notice a nice circle around my desk. Shooing everyone away, I slowly came face to face with Kelly. She was not so happy.

"Hey, Kelly, what up?"

"Well, perky ass! Remember those billionaire clients that wanted to seal the deal?"

"Wanted? They don't want to anymore?"

"No, they still want it, but they don't want me as their rep!"

"Well then who do they want?!"

"YOU!"

"So what does that mean?"

"That means you get the commission! And I GET NOTHING!"

As Kelly started to cry, all I could hear were *cha-ching* sounds! I saw myself on the beach and so much more!

"THAT'S AWESOME!"

"Congrats, you're rich, bitch."

147

"So how many figures is this account? And the VP position?"

"Ugh, rub it in my face! They signed a two-point-five million dollar deal."

"And here at Sharps we get how much for commission?"

"Forty-five percent commission."

"Meaning?" I already knew how much it was; I just wanted to hear her say it.

"One million one hundred twenty-five thousand dollars."

"And when will this be in my account?"

"By the first of next month."

"Hey, Kelly?"

"Yeah?"

"SUCK IT!"

As I rubbed our biggest client's account in my manager's face, I had never felt better. Now I knew why she wanted that account, why she was hassling me to bust my ass while she did absolutely nothing! I was told that this account was a mere couple thousand at first because the billionaires were prospective clients. I guess they loved me and all my knowledge and they decided to trust in us 100 percent and invest more. Wow, so I did have the gall, the balls, or whatever choice of words you would like to use. This proved that I was unstoppable! Now what should I do with my newfound riches?

The rest of the day was going by great so far. Kelly stopped sobbing and looked at the bright side of things. To her, now Sharps would be up and running longer because of this huge client. This one client would be able to support this whole business for at least a few more years. She later came to my desk with a big smile.

"Hey, gal pal!"

"Hello, Satan."

"So what are you doing tonight?"

"Watching movies, drinking wine, and farting, why?"

"Well that sounds like fun! I love your plans, you're so cool."

"What do you want, Kelly."

"Well, let's hang, now since you're rich, you're almost like me. Not as cute, though, but you have money. Trust me, us girls who have money needs to stick together."

Well I didn't want to be alone tonight,. Richie was busy working late and Jen was with her new love match; Ray was out of state and Sean would most likely be experimenting with my car. And hey, I did need a ride home, anyways.

"Okay, sure. After work?"

"Yeah! Oh, you wanna get your nails done? Your hands are looking a little butch."

Looking down at my hands, I slowly nodded my head. Maybe some gal time with Kelly wouldn't be bad; she could teach me about nails and so forth.

Nail Salon = Drama Time

"Okay, so check this out, peeps, I'm here in the salon about to get my nails done!" I said frantically, talking to Sean and Ray on the phone.

"Really?" said Ray.

"Why? Did you bite them too short and they started to bleed again?" asked Sean.

"NO, dip dong! Kelly asked me to go so I agreed." The phone went silent for a while, so I wasn't too sure what was going on inside my friends' heads. "HELLO! Why is it so quiet! I'm freaking out here!"

"Wow, so you won't let your best friend drag you into a nail place, but you'll go with Kelly?" said Ray.

"Huh?"

"He's implying your BFF, as in Jen."

"I know what he's talking about, Sean, I just don't

know what that, aka Jen, has to do with me getting my nails did!"

"Well, seeing how you and Jen have been quite snippy lately and you've been dodging all of us to hang out with your new boy toy, I believe Jen has a lot more to do with this than you think."

"Hope, you're speaking in acronyms!" yelled Sean

"and not to mention your attitude has been sucking!' said Ray

"You've been ditzy, mean, rude, MEAN and you keep ignoring your true friends! I mean--"

"Ugh, whatever guys, thanks for nothing! Barbie is on the way in, I gots to go!"

Hanging up the phone on my two mesties (male besties), I felt bad, but hey, a girl has to do what she has to do anyways, right?

"H to the O to the P to the E! Hope you don't mind, but I brought some gal pals."

"Kelly! Hey!"

"So are you ready to get sexified and talk shit?"

"Excuse me?"

"In all salons, whether it be nail or hair or even tanning, it's justified girl time, aka Operation Vent. Release and wrap it up with a little shit talk."

"Okay, I see!"

"So do you wanna dish, or should I?"

There I was, sitting in a room full of nail polish fumes, fake boobed women, and yeah, you guessed it, gossip, now faced with the tough question: her or me?

"Okay, since you're taking too long—" Insert awkward giggle among her friends. "—I'll start first. So my brother the fag hag is just a complete and utter mess. I mean, he's literally trying to sue me!!"

"Great choice of words, Kelly," said Bimbo Number Three, aka Shana.

"Why, thanks! I've been looking up all these new words and terminology because I don't want to seem like a dipstick in the name of the Justice League."

"Oh, that makes sense!" Bimbo Number Two, aka Lauren, said.

"The name of the Justice League?" I said, and then all the girls giggled and laughed.

"OMG, Hope! Yeah, the Justice League? Like when they say, 'Stop in the name of the justice?' They mean to say Justice League and they just cut it short."

"Okay, Kelly, no, that's 'Stop in the name of the law.'"

"Duh! The law as in Justice League!"

As her dimwitted friends rolled their eyes at me and nodded their heads towards Kelly, I saw I was outnumbered and just agreed. As the girls continued to trash talk, cry, and do god knows what, an hour rolled by and it was my turn to dish. Jen was calling, and I didn't want to answer because, well, I would tell her where I was, at so I hit *Ignore*.

"So, Hope."

"Yes, Kelly?"

"Now tell me, that cute, hunky, tall-dark-and-sexy man-friend of yours. You hit that?" All the girls smiled and looked and me with cat clock eyes!

Sitting there stunned by the question, I shakily said, "No."

They all gasped and stared at each other. "Why not?!" asked Bimbo Number One, aka Shelly.

"Well because he is my friend, and I don't bang my friends. You're not supposed to."

"Said who?!" asked Kelly. "Man, if I had that hunk of man meat in my presence, I would tear that UP! And then I would—"

"KELLY! Okay, I get it!"

"Oh, sorry, I got ahead of myself," she said, fixing her hair and adjusting her blouse. "So what about Jen?"

"Have I had sex with Jen?!" I asked slowly, getting

pissed.

"Oh, heck no! She's way out of your league. I'm talking about the deal with Jen. I don't see her coming to the office as much anymore. You're not glued to your phone texting her like you used to be, and I've had no reason to intercept your phone lines and listen in on your convos. So yeah, what's up with you two?"

"Wait, you listen to me while I'm on the phone?! Anyways, well, she's just been bitchy lately." That's all I said as I kept reading my *People* magazine.

"And?!" Kelly nudged.

"And so we don't talk as much?" I said with an inflection.

"HOPE! Gosh, this is when you DISH! You go into details, you express yourself."

I sat there in the pedicure chair, with the bimbos and Kelly looking at me and Jen sending me a text message, thinking to myself, *I think this all might backfire, but it would be nice to get this all off my chest.* I took another two minutes pretending to be interested in the Bieber and Selena Gomez split. I finally came out from the magazine, took a deep breath, and said what was on my mind.

"Well, she's just a douche. She's acting like a dick lately. And honestly, I think it's because I have a man and she doesn't. I think it's because I'm moving forward in my job and she isn't."

"Oooh, juicy! So you think it's just ultimate jealousy?"

"Yeah, pretty much. I think she's mad that she can't get a man like Richie and that she wants my life. And Ray, he's all about love, but he just whores it up! His emotions, I mean. Jen is the physical whore and Ray is the emotional whore. He doesn't know how to slow down, and honestly, he's a big, clingy crybaby! And Sean, ugh, he knows it all! Or at least tries to! So I always think to myself, if you know it all why are you so miserable and alone?"

"Okay, all dry!" said the nail tech, talking about my toes. Kelly sat there looking way too interested in what I was talking about. Her friends had a smug grin on their faces, and something in my gut was telling me I shouldn't have said any of that.

"Well, Hopester, we should all do dinner or get drinks sometime. Tell Mr. Richie I say *hola*."

Then that was that; Kelly and her posse walked out of the nail salon and talked amongst each other. I guess I could head home now?

155

* * *

Dear Diary,

Today was strange. I got the nails done with Kelly and her friends. They sucked me into talking about Jen and my friends. And honestly it felt good to speak about what's on my chest; I just hope I didn't say this to the wrong person....
Goodnight.
<3 Hope.

Strange Actions

Okay, so that night when I got home, Jen wasn't
there. She is usually humping something or watching TV. It
was super strange! Anywho, I woke up and still no Jen! Was
I already starting to feel guilty for talking to Kelly? Had I
really understood that going to do something so harmless—
aka getting my nails done—with someone else instead of Jen
was so horrible? And lastly, was Jen really jealous of my
life? I mean, we hardly talked anymore so I didn't know what
was going on with her.

As I took my morning stroll to the bathroom, it was
quiet and lonely. I sat on the poop pot, no singing this time,
just drowning in my own thoughts, hoping to hear a door
creak open so I could at least say hi to Jen. Fifteen minutes
on the pot, no pee or poo, no door creaks, no TV turned on.
Instead just a text from Kelly.

"Hey girlfriend! It was great to chit chat see you this
morn!"

Taking a deep breath, I sent back a smiley face and
said, *Right on!* I then closed my text messages and opened
my Bang app on my phone. I had five more friend requests
and a couple more messages, one being from Richie. He
seemed to have lost his phone while on his business trip. That

would explain why I hadn't heard from him the night before. I wrote back with a winky face and a *See you tonight*. That was just the right amount of love I needed to wake me up this morning.

Right when I had a smile on my face, the door slammed open. There she was, right in the doorway, smiling like she'd just gotten a brand new puppy, a big bottle of protein, and a new car.

"Jen?"

"Yes, yes that 'tis my name."

"Oh, lord. Soo, what's up?"

"Just had the best night ever with my Mr. Sexy."

"REALLY!? I totally forgot about that."

'Totally?" Since when did you start using that word?"

"Well, umm, since Kelly and I—"

"Alright, who cares about her. Anywho, my night was amazing. We sat up all night and—"

"Humped?"

"No! We talked. That's right, pure conversation. I've never been more turned on in my life! There's something sexy about hearing a guy who actually knows what he is talking about. Ya know?"

"Yes, I def know! Well, that is totes awesome!"

"Since you forgot what I was doing last night even

though I've been talking about it for days, what did you do? Wait did you just sat totes?"

Okay, here was the big question. I could've lied and said, "Oooh, nothing, just watched Lifetime," or I could've said, "I went out with Richie," or I could've said, "I fell asleep!" But instead I told the truth. The painful truth.

"I went and got my nails and feet done—" There it was, the blank stare. "—with Kelly and the bimbos?" My eyes squinted and my voice went a whole four octaves higher.

"Oh, so you ignored my calls and texts and you won't go with me to get your nails done, but the moment the bimbo skanky squad asks you, you do it?"

"Well, Jen, it's not like—"

"Convo done."

The door slammed and there I was, still left on the pot. Today was going to be a great day! Great, Hope, you def know how to put your foot in your mouth this time, don't cha?

After sitting on the pot all by my lonesome, I finally decided to get up and get ready for work. Was I really that bad? Sure, I'd gotten a few highlights and gotten my nails done more than often. I was a little addicted to my phone and

Bang, but hey, that was normal, right? After a 40-minute beauty routine, I was finally ready for work. Getting into my car, I felt a little lonely and uneasy. For once my car ride to work was smooth going—the doors worked, the radio was fine, and it ran as smooth as a new car—but all I wanted was a little quiet.

Entering into Sharps, I thought the days seemed to be changing. People were staring at me and weren't as friendly as they used to be. I got to my desk and turned on my computer, pulled up my Microsoft programs, and turned on my internet radio. Right when I was winding down and settling into my workspace, I was met by Kelly's face.

"Hopekins! Hey, girl! What cha doin'?"

"Hey, Kelly, I'm just about to start workin'."

"Hahahhhahaha! Oh my gosh, you are soo cute! So how was your night? You talk to Richie? Have a little phone you-know-what?"

"Umm, phone sex? No, my night was chill, relaxed."

"Then why are you so, blah, you know, down?"

"Well it's Jen, she—"

"Hopekins, you need to drop her—she's poison—and just hang with me. She's gonna, you know, drag you down and throw you in the bus."

"You mean under the bus, and no, she wouldn't do that."

"What makes you so sure?"

"Because she's my best friend."

"Well, Hope, sorry to burst your bubble, but you are supposed to be her bestie, and you replaced her with me."

"Not true."

"Oh really? Well when was the last time you guys spent some BFF time together? Ate lunch? Dished on gossip or got your nails done? For the past couple months, it's been with me. Let's just face it, you're my mini!" Kelly smiled and walked away with such confidence it made me sick. I was sitting there contemplating, *Am I really confident in Jen and me? Am I really turning into a mini Kelly?* I had way too many thoughts on my mind. I had a full day of work ahead of me, and this distraction that Kelly had brought was not helping. But then again, was it really a distraction or the truth?

After about three hours of working and not looking up from my computer, I had to take a break. I walked over to the water dispenser to ponder some more thoughts. I grabbed a paper cup and started to pour myself some water. I sat down by the dispenser, rolled my neck hoping it would pop, closed my eyes, and inhaled a nice big breath. When I turned

161

around, Beth was right in my face.

"DAMN IT, BETH!"

"Oh, sorry Kell— I mean Hope. You looked so peaceful I didn't want to ask you to move, so I was just trying to reach around you."

"It's okay, you just scared me. And did you almost call me Kelly?"

"Well, yeah."

"Why?"

"Because you look just like her, and you're starting to be mean like her, too."

"No I'm not."

"Hope, we all miss the old you. The nice girl who ate with us instead of this one who pokes fun at us. We miss the Hope who had intellect and deep conversation, not the one who giggles and flips her hair with the bimbo twins. You've changed a lot."

Beth stopped talking and looked me in my face. I flipped her cup of water in the air and stomped my little butt to Kelly's office. I was heated, pissed, mad, upset. All I could see was red. Approaching Kelly's semi-shut door, I began to open it but then decided to eavesdrop on another conversation.

"My favorite cousin! Did you seal the deal? Well you

have to because I need her as weak as I can. You make your moves on both of them and keep trying to separate the two. When you do, she is bound to confide in me and I can dig up enough dirt to let her go. I need this account and I can't have it solo if she is still here, got it? The party is this weekend, so we need to move ASAP. I want her gone by Monday before Daddy comes to visit!"

I backed up a little from the door because this seemed like a conversation that I shouldn't be listening to. I went back to my desk in a little tiff, wondering what Kelly was talking about. What account? Who did she want gone? What party, and why wasn't I invited? Someone had better not be throwing a party the same day as mine.

As I continued to work, I looked at the clock and saw it was almost lunch time. I went to the kitchen to see what I had, in hopes that I'd left something there from before. When that avenue came up dry, I proceeded to look online and see who could deliver. After searching numerous menus, I got a text from Richie, who wanted to know if I'd eaten yet. Man, this guy was a savior. I replied no, and he said he would bring me lunch and that he'd be here in 30 minutes.

I tried to type away and be busy, but my stomach was killing me. I was on Bang, replying to some messages and friend requests while liking some of Kelly's pictures she'd posted of her and me. Something told me to go through Kelly's old albums, so I did. I came across one titled *Family Bahamas and Friends 2011.* Clicking through, I saw a happy Kelly and her brother Matt. More pictures of her family, and then I came across one that looked like my Richie, but this guy had really black hair and green eyes. I guess everyone does have a twin out there, huh? Before I knew it, Richie was looking at me, hovering over my desk.

"Hey there, starving Marvin, ready to eat?"

"Hey, honey! I sure am. Let's go downstairs, I need to talk to you."

"You okay?"

"Kinda, just a little venting session is in order."

"Okay, gorgeous, let's go."

As Richie and I headed downstairs I couldn't help but smile and feel an instant happiness. We sat down at the table that was the furthest away from any kind of civilization.

"Okay, hot stuff, what's bothering you?"

"Well, I kind of talked to Jen this morning, and we got into a little spat. She accused me of changing, then Kelly called me her Mini-Me, and Beth said I was just like Kelly, and the boys are angry because of how I treated Jen, and everyone wants me to apologize! But for what? I don't see a problem."

"Wow, and all this happened in the span of what, four, maybe five hours?"

"Yes."

"Well, do you think you've changed?"

"Well, a little, but not a lot. Like, ever since they made me get a Bang account, I've found myself liking being girly, and a little bitchy because I can stand up for myself and not be a pushover. But I don't see me as being over the top."

"Well maybe they see something you don't. You have to roll with the punches, champ, and see and really listen to what others are saying. Take it into consideration. Take a step back and love yourself. Don't stress too much over it."

This man knew what to say and how to say it. He was right on so many levels, so I supposed I could take his advice and give myself a double-take. We finished up lunch, he gave me a kiss, and I went back to work. After that pep talk I felt like I could take on the whole day.

Before I knew it, the time read five o'clock and it was time to clock out and go home. I got up from my cubical and noticed that I was the only one left in the office. Kelly had left early, and I supposed everyone else had followed suit.

Walking to my car, I slowly put my key into the door and threw my stuff on the passenger seat. I plopped my overworked body in my seat and rested my head on my steering wheel. The parking lot was empty. I watched a coyote battle a squirrel, a skateboarder eat shit trying to jump over my car, and an old lady chase a paper bag, yelling at it for littering. After my comical rest I started up ol' faithful and headed home.

Maybe I should leave work late every day; there was hardly any traffic. I hit every green light and I was home in no time. Reaching my door, I walked in, happy and relaxed, to a quiet home.

I started up my bath and soon soaked my whole body, played some smooth music, and placed cucumbers over my eyes.

* * *

Dear Diary,

I need help.

<3 The Confused Hope

Birthday Planning!

It had been a couple weeks since Jen and I had talked, let alone seen each other. Either I was out with Richie or working, or she was out with her mystery beau or sleeping. Our paths seemed to no longer connect.

On waking up I did my normal: checked Bang, saw my texts, and hit snooze five more times. This time while waking up I saw Ray and Sean right in my face.

"ATHENA!" shouted Sean.

"What up, big butt?!" said Ray.

"Hey, guys."

"So any plans on what to do for Saturday?"

"What's Saturday?" I asked, then Sean and Ray slowly looked at each other. Ray lifted his arm and felt my forehead.

"Really, Athena? You have been busy, huh? First you were all excited about it for the past couple months, and it's like we never see you and you just forget?"

"Sean, Ray, what are you talking about?"

"YOUR BIRTHDAY!" they said in unison. I sat up looked at the calendar. I had totally forgotten about my birthday! I stared at the circled date and back at Sean and Ray.

"OOOH MY GOSH! How can I forget my own birthday!? So I have NOTHING—and I mean nothing—planned! Jen and I were—"

"Supposed to go over the deets, we know," interrupted Sean.

"You've been ignoring all your friends, and we hear it's because you have a new lady friend, aka Kelly," implied Ray.

"What makes you say that?"

"Jen told us," Sean said. Shit, things get around faster than Kim Kardashian!

"Well, you know, it's just that—"

Ray put his hand up and shook his head. "That's why she was calling you yesterday and texting. You two had a date to make plans for your party."

"Damn it! I'm so stupid! UGH!"

"It's okay, she went ahead and planned something. Food, décor, place, and times, just for you. So it's all planned out, and Ray and I approved, so you have nothing to do but get all dressed up and show up."

"Wow, she did all that for me?"

"You're her best friend, she knows you best, so it wasn't too hard. So don't worry about it, Athena, it's under control."

"I thought she hated me?"

"Well, she does," said Ray. "But she's not a flake."

"Apologize. Get it out of the way so we all can hang again."

"Yeah. We miss you, so come on, get it together," said Ray.

The boys left the house, leaving me in thought. But this morning I was happy. My birthday was Saturday and my bestie had figured it all out for me. I skipped and smiled all morning while getting ready and eating breakfast. Driving to work, I couldn't help but smile. This morning was off to a great start! Only thing that would make it better would be seeing Jen so I could apologize and give her a big hug. Walking into Sharps, I had pep in my step. My BFF wasn't too mad at me, since she'd taken this big task off my hands.

"Hey, Hope!" yelled Kelly. I waved excitedly at her, and you know she had to come over and see what was up. "So, you are extra chipper, my little dipper! What's going on?"

"Well I forgot my birthday is next weekend and I was supposed to meet with Jen to go over the deets and—"

"Okay, cut this story short. I need to twirl my hair."

"Okay, okay, so Jen took over the menu, place, music, and times—all of that—so all I have to do is show up!"

"So, she won't have anything too fattening on the menu, right? Like meats and carbs? Because you know, Hope, you do have a little bit of chubs coming out on your sides. I'd avoid those if I were you."

"You are totally right! Well I hope she doesn't. I'm sure she will have an awesome selection."

Sitting at work smiling, I went automatically onto my Bang account, posted a little heart on my love's profile, accepted a few more friend requests, and posted some more duck face pictures. Let's face it, I wasn't going to really work today; I had birthday brain! I decided to get my head out of my ass and text Jen. I whipped out my phone and stared at it for 10 minutes. I had no idea how to start off the text. *"Hey Jen, want to meet at the house after work? The boys came by and told me all about the planning. I owe you one"* *<3 Hope*

After waiting another ten minutes for a response, she replied with: *Sure.*

Sure was my reply? Okay, I'd take it. At least she'd replied, right?

Party for Review

After work, I got a text from Jen saying she would be late, so I decided to hop in a bath early. A nice twenty-minute bath was all I needed. I got up and looked in the mirror. I couldn't help but do some poses and wave to my adoring crowd, aka my shampoo and conditioner.

"Who is a sexy bitch?! Oh yeah, that's right, I am!" I squinted my eyes, flipped my hair, sang LMFAO, and rocked out. It wasn't long before I started to hear hands slowly clapping and someone whistling. Turning around too fast, I slipped on the bathroom floor mat.

"How long were you there?"

"Well I walked by as you were singing LMFAO, I couldn't—no wait, I wouldn't dare to miss this awesome concert. I was about to fight the shampoo bottle for her spot. Seems like the best seat in the house."

"Ha, ha, just help me up, please?"

Reaching down to grab my hand, Jen reluctantly helped me up.

"So you ready to speak b-day?!" Jen said.

"OF COURSE! And I'm really sorry about not answering your text and call, and I'm also sorry about not telling you I was getting a mani and pedi with Kelly."

"Mani and pedi, wow. Your word usage is slowly

changing to a girl's more and more every day."

As we walked out of the bathroom, I was greeted with another round of applause. Ray and Sean were hootin' and hollerin', screaming, "Encore!" I couldn't help but roll my eyes and speed walk to the kitchen.

"Okay, so for the first order of business," Ray began, "your performance was mediocre. I bet five dollars Sean can out-sing you and teach you a few things."

"Second order for today, I vote to remove all bathroom floor mats," added Sean.

"And for the third thing for today, I v ote that Hope, after this meeting and after she gets beat by Sean, walks outside in her underwear and screams, 'Will you touch my wiener?'" said Jen.

"All in favor say aye?" said Sean.

"Okay, okay! Shut it up! Ray and Sean, I accept the challenge, and Jen, if I lose, I accept my defeat. Now for the fourth motion, give me the list of ideas for this shindig."

Jen, Sean, and Ray looked so excited to show me this; they all giggled in unison and gave me the paper. I looked it over and couldn't help but keep Kelly in my mind when it came to her ideas about food and music and so forth. The food menu and the music playlist looked great! But this party was also a time for me to network and build my career.

"Okay, so pen?" I snapped, and Sean gave me his, out of his shirt pocket. I began to cross things off the list and proceeded to hand it back.

"So what's this?" asked Jen.

"Oh, no biggie," I said as I grabbed my phone to text Kelly. "Just the marked-off things need to be changed." They all zoomed in on the list and looked at me like I was crazy.

"Athena, everything is crossed off the list."

"Exactly!" I said.

"So you want us to redo everything?"

"Yeah, I mean the food is great, but you know, like Kelly said, I have to watch my weight. The music selection is awesome too, but I'm not sure about how people would take in Sir Mix-a-Lot. So it's just a few minor chang—"

"Kelly said this? And Kelly said that?!" implied Ray.

"Who are you texting now?" asked Jen as I began to laugh loudly at the funny things Kelly was saying.

"Hello?! Who are you texting?" asked Jen again.

"Oh, it's just Kelly, she is hilarious! She was just implying that you would like the menu because of your hippo thighs!! Hahahaha, hippo! And you're not like a hippo, more like rhino. Man, the things she says!"

"You know what, Kelly?"

"Um, it's Hope, Jen."

173

"No, she got it right the first time," said Ray.

"You are a bitch. A downright spoiled brat. I don't know what happened to you or my friend, but she is not here. You can have your Kelly and her friends and her life, you can have not eating carbs and talking shit about people. But what you won't have is me as a friend. I'll be moving out by the end of the month. Happy fucking birthday."

Ray, Sean, and Jen all looked at me in disgust. Jen got all teary-eyed and walked out, slamming things and tearing up the paper. Ray and Sean continued to look at me as if I were an object in a museum.

"Wow, Hope, that was cold."

"Straight rude, Athena!"

"Well she needs to up her game a little. It's okay, she will fix it. I don't know what her problem is. She should be lucky that she's even invited to my birthday! It's an honor to breath my air"

"Serious?" asked Ray "Who says that?"

"Do you not hear what anyone else has to say but yourself or Kelly? Do you not listen? She just told you what her problem was, and honestly it's not just her problem, it's mine and Sean's' also."

"Damn, Hope, just fix this," said Sean.

* * *

Dear Diary,

So I don't know what came over me! I was a total
bitch to Jen, but like Kelly said, some people don't like
change and at times you have to give it to them? Man, I hope
taking Kelly's advice is the right thing to do.
<3 Hop

Ray and Sean are Pissy!

Today I decided to go into work late. I had a lot to
think about: I'd been rude to Jen; my party seemed like it was
going to be a bust; I'd never heard back on that VP position;
and my love, Richie, was out of state, so I couldn't see that
gorgeous face. Today screamed *Give Hope a Little Bit of*
Hope Day. A day full of Lifetime TV, ice cream, chips, and
sweatpants. But first I was going to kick it off with a bubble
bath.

Walking to the bathroom, I noticed Jen's room was
empty. I could hear the cat clock ticking loudly and the water
from the faucet dripping. This must've been what it was like
for Bella in *Twilight* when she finally turned into a vampire. I
looked into the mirror and rubbed my gorgeous face, walked
to the tub and turned on the water. Soon it was warm enough,
and then it was time for me to go bubble crazy.

I sat in the tub, contemplating my own thoughts, with phone in hand. I know—I was supposed to relax, but I couldn't help but see if Richie had texted me or if I'd gotten any new messages or friend requests on Bang. Like I'd already known: five more requests and more messages. I thought I should change my picture. Right now it was of me with a sexy-ass duck face, boobs out, and makeup on. I looked hella hot! Okay, enough of the phone; it was time to put this away.

I locked the cellular device, placed it on the counter, lit some candles, and played my Pandora playlist of Grace and the Nocturnals. Closing my eyes, I could swear I heard voices, and no, not like *Psycho* movie voices, but real, human voices. I sat up in the tub and the voices stopped, along with the footsteps. Laying back down and closing my eyes, I then opened my eyes 10 minutes later to a very mad Ray and Sean.

"HOLY SHIT! What the hell, you guys! What do you want?! And does anyone know where the doorbell is?"

"S'up, Athena, we want to talk to you. And the doorbell is on the right side of your front door. Unless you're looking out, and then it's on the left."

"Ugh, Sean, good morning. Oh, how I missed your

sarcasm."

"Hey, hey, hey! No need to be rude to Sean! You've used all your asshole cards!" yelled Ray.

"UGH! Sorry! What do you want?" I moaned.

"Well, Athena Asshole, you need to apologize to Jen."

"Why?" I said as I folded my arms.

"Because, Pouty Barbie, she busted her ass and worked her schedule around yours, booked halls and grabbed décor just for you, gathered the menu, and your ungrateful, newly spoiled ass was rude."

"Yeah, and you didn't even say thank you," added Sean.

"I know. Well, she obviously doesn't know me to grab the things she did, so she had it coming, and—"

"Enough," Ray said as he put his hand up high. "She knows you well. Very well. Not to mention she used her savings just for you Sean, let's go."

"Hey, Athena, the question is, do you know who you are?" Sean said as half his body was out of the bathroom door. "Ever since you got a little money and started hanging out with your new BFF, you lost site of Hope. And so did we, pun intended."

"Hope, last night got pretty heated and a little rough

for all of us. Things were said and feelings were hurt. All she did was help someone who continues to be a bitch to her. Why? Because she's a real friend and she loves you."

"Good point, muscles, now Athena, just fix it."

They walked out of the bathroom, closing the door. There I was, alone now, and I'd never felt more miserable. There was no way I could be alone. off to work I went.

Outcasting it at Work

For some reason, every time I walked into the office I always got strange looks. Some people would look at me and quickly turn away , others would pretend I didn't exist, and the rest just ran the other way. It was like I was walking in slow motion and my hair was floating in the air, with a big, bright light behind me. Oh well. I didn't know what they wanted or what they were scared of. Do you think it had to do with me hanging out with Kelly?

I walked past Kelly's office and she was in a deep conversation yet again. Her Botox was starting to wear because you could see her wrinkles coming back; that's how I figured out this convo was something serious.

"I don't care! Do what you have to do. I already told you, I need this and her to be brought down ASAP! I have to go, Hope is in the doorway. Remember what I said."

"Hey, doll!"

"Hey, Kells!"

"Aw, Kells? I love it! Hugzies!"

"So who was that? Seemed pretty intense."

"Oh, just my cousin Ri— Ronald. You know, family issues."

"So I was thinking, maybe today we can go get pho."

"Oooh, Hope, that sounds yummy! By the way, your new client will be in today, so you want to take them along?"

"Of course! They are only giving me over a million dollars!"

We both embraced in a laugh while flipping our hair all over the place. I sat at my desk and Kells walked slowly towards her office. I flipped my hair some more and looked in my mini pocket mirror to check my hair and makeup. I sat at my desk and spun in my chain. I then opened my web browser and jumped on Bang.

Nothing new so far: some more pictures had been liked; no one had liked any of my posts about my thoughts and politics; but I did have some more messages! Man, is this what it felt like to be Kells and Jen? To be so hot and get so much attention was just exhausting!

"Okay, everyone! Let's all head into the meeting room!" said Kelly as her little Smurfs headed in, one by one.

I was surprised that we had a meeting today. There hadn't been an email, nothing marked on my calendar, and Kells hadn't mentioned anything. I did as the rest and hopped my butt into the meeting room.

"Okay, first thing's first, some of you might not know, but Hope got us a huge account that will allow us to bring on some more people and do some possible raises! So with that being said, my aunts have suckered me into hiring back my brother, so...everyone please welcome back Matt!"

Everyone stood up and started clapping. The room filled with happiness, which had seemed to be missing since Matt was canned in the first place.

"Thank you! Thank you! Oh, Beth, have you lost weight? Steve, your hair is growing back so nicely. And ummm...who are you?" Matt asked, pointing to me.

"Matt! Silly billy! It's me! Hope!"

"Oh, wow, don't you look like Hope."

He looked me up and down in disgust with his flaming pink ascot and walked past me. Kelly? Was this true? Sure, I loved my makeup and such, but whatever. He was just jealous that I'd gotten a huge account and he wouldn't get any of the goods.

"Okay, so like I said, Matt is back and I'm very excited about this," said Kelly.

"Eh-hum!" Matt cleared his throat very loudly.

"Okay, and I've been wanting to hire a VP of the company. Do we need it? No, but—"

Cough, cough. Matt scratched his throat even louder.

"But it's in my nature to want to widen the love of Sharps and the possibilities it can reach. I was going to hire from within, but it was insisted that I bring in Matt as my VP."

The whole room gasped and looked at me. One of the big deals was that I'd been promised the spot as VP when I nabbed that big account, and we'd been spending bestie time together, and so much more! My heart was officially broken.

Walking out of the meeting, my co-workers were staring at me and talking. Matt came to my desk, trying his best to grab my attention.

"So I know you and Kelly have been FBFFs, bu—

"FBFFs?" I asked.

"Yeah, fake best friends forever. Anywho, back to what I was saying. I understand the whole FBFFs thing, but let's face it, she is a shark and you're like a guppy and she just ate you. Have a great day!"

Matt skipped away from my desk and into his new corner office with the view and shades, while I sat there like a sad puppy. Before I could even turn around, Kelly was right at my desk.

"Hey, sista, want to do lunch?"

"Yeah, sure,"

"You okay, Hope?"

"No, but we will talk about this at lunch. Are you driving or me?"

"Please, me be seen in your dirt wagon? Haha, you're silly! I'll drive."

Kelly grabbed her bag and we headed to her car. Trying to figure out which pho place to go to, we finally made a decision. Walking into the restaurant, I let Kelly talk her little head off because in my head I was preparing to ask so many questions.

"So do you know what you're going to get?" Kelly said, staring at me as I was caught looking into the abyss. "HOPE!"

"Oh, what? Yeah, I'm getting the pho."

"Yeah, I know that, we are at a pho restaurant, question is, what kind?"

"I don't care, pick for me." I replied.

"So what's new?"

"A lot actually, Kells." I began to tell her about the problems with the boys and Jen. I told her about the party and the menu and that I demanded it to be changed.

"Girl, who cares?! Don't worry about the rejct squad, you're in with the in crowd now. Welcome to the land of money and success. You are too good for those kind, just step into the world of luxury without feeling guilty." Kelly stated.

"Yeah, I know, and ugh! They make me so mad! Like, why should I feel bad for speaking the truth? For telling them how it is? And hey, that's life...tough shit!"

"That's the thing, Hopekins, small people don't understand."

"They get jealous easy. I mean they wntd me to change"

"I know, boo! It's okay, we are soul sisters now."

"So, what happened to that VP position?"

"Well, I know. My family threatened to take the biz away if I didn't bring Matt back on."

"So why not just tell me?"

"Because I didn't want to lose a friend."

So when had I started getting regular manis and pedis with Kelly? Since my friends had ditched me and couldn't take the truth. Hey, Kelly wasn't so bad; she actually had a little soul in there. Now, I said "little," not a huge gigantic one. It was like she understood me and got what I was going through. I was slowly getting closer to her; the way I talked and how I dressed was so Kelly. Everything she said was so funny, and I couldn't help but recite some of her sayings as well. I mean, she was awesome!

"Oh, yeah. So, Kelly, you've been pretty intense lately at work. What's going on?"

"What you mean?"

"Well, your secret phone calls and having your door shut. And today you forgot your lipstick."

"Oh, that?" she said as she giggled hideously loudly. "That's nothing, just nothing."

"So if it's nothing, want to dish on that?"

"Oh, well, can't really. Just a plan I'm creating to get rid of a few bad eggs."

We sat and ate our pho and I listened very closely to what Kelly had to say. For some reason something didn't seem right; I felt like this plan she was hatching would hit closer to home. Soon her phone rang and Kelly left the table. I couldn't make out what she was saying since she was pretty far away. I pretended to be going to the rest room, so I squeezed past Kelly and put my ear up to the wall.

"Hey there cousin, did you get the audio I sent you? GOOD! Look I need all the dirt I can on Hope. Get into her house, find shit out. Platy dirty, we only have a couple of days to pull this off."

Kelly walked back to the table and I went into the bathroom. What could she be talking about? What dirt? Walking back to the table I smiled at Kelly who was smiling so big back at me.

"Interesting phone call huh?"

"What do you mean?"

"I mean the one you just had about getting dirt on me?"

"Oh that! PSH! It's nothing"

"Okay I don't think getting dirt on someone is nothing"

"Okay here's the deal. I need to know all the dirt on you because we just signed our biggest client and if I don't know EVERYTHING about you first they will and they could possible cancel our deal"

"Makes sense"

"See nothing fishy.... Just pure business. So you ready to go?"

"Yeah.."

Dear Diary,
Something doesn't feel right
<3 the nervous Hope.

Hope's Wrath

Okay, I get it; I'm changing. Bang is taking over my entire being as a woman, I'm losing grip on my friends, my family are what I have left, and my job...well, I'm succeeding, but I'm becoming Kelly's bestie. To make matters worse, I've been on my period for the past week! Doctor says it's because of my hormones, the amounts of sex that I am not having, stress at work, and friends. My body is pretty much saying, *Screw you*.

I woke up this morning and my ovaries were in an episode of *Celebrity Death Match*, Hulk vs. Hulkimania, and I'll tell ya, I was the one who was losing. Then I had to give a semi-big presentation. I had to also stay on Kelly's ass about this promotion, too.

Walking to my car, I kicked a squirrel, got attacked by a cat, and I believe I saw a raccoon mean-mug me. Lord, what did I do? Mother Nature sure is being a mother fucker, and I'm the one who's getting it all.

Once I was in the car, it wouldn't start, my radio wouldn't turn down, and my door, for the love of all that is human, wouldn't shut. So there I was, putt-putting on the highway, blasting Prince on the radio, and my door was opening and shutting, causing all the other cars to swerve.

Usually I would call Jen and she would make a joke to make me feel better, but right now I had no one but myself.

Being stuck at a red light for about six minutes, I whipped out my phone and checked Bang. To make me feel better, I responded to some messages about how hot I am. I didn't know what had gotten into me lately, but when I spoke about myself I instantly got happy. So there I was, smiling in cyberspace, when in reality I had a million horns honking at me.

When I got to work, my door finally decided to shut and stay that way, so I had to crawl out my window. By doing so, I caught the only small piece of crap that was hanging on my window and ripped my tights and skirt. So now my hair was a mess, my pantyhose were ripped, and my skirt looked like shit. Walking into my building, I ran to catch the elevator and fell flat on my face. Once I got up I realized I'd broken the right heel of my shoe. So now, rip in the tights, skirt torn, hair a mess, could hardly hear, and I was limping due to my broken heel. It's safe to say, I looked like a prostitute or one of Tiger Woods's mistresses.

Getting to my desk, I sat down to what seemed to take me an eternity to reach. I turned on my computer and nothing happened. I fidgeted with my mouse, and still a black screen. Unplugged my computer and plugged it back in, still nothing.

So in return I flipped my desk, screamed like Tarzan's chimp, threw my papers in the air, and hauled my chair across the office.

"Umm, hey, Hope?...Hopikens? HOPE!"

"Oh, hi, Kelly."

"Yeah, um, hey, you look ugly. I can't have that here, so go home."

"Kelly, I'm fine, I can work today."

"I bet you can, sport, but not looking like this. I want clients who walk into my office to not be scared of Sasquatch sitting outside of it. Pack your things and go home."

Looking around, I noticed I was scaring my co-workers. Betty was ducking behind my cubical wall, Steve was in the corner crying, and others were army crawling, hoping I wouldn't see them. So I nodded, grabbed what little dignity I had left, and went home.

When I got home I sat another day in silence. I grabbed my phone and wanted to vent and talk to someone so bad, but I'd driven all my friends away. So that left the people who are supposed to be there no matter what: family. I picked up the phone and told my mom I was headed over.

Family Reassurance

"So, Mom, do you think I'm in the wrong? I mean, yes, I should have invited Jen at least and hey, it's my boss. What was I supposed to do?"

"Well, love bug, you didn't have to talk about your friends like you did. They are your friends and they are the ones who are there for you. And plus, didn't you always say Kelly is the root of evil?"

"Yeah."

"So then why try your hardest to fit in?"

"Well, because it's my job."

"No, honey, it's not your job to fit in. It's your job to be the best damn rep at Sharps, not to be the BFF to the head of the company while shitting on all your real friends."

"Thanks, Mom."

"You're welcome, love. Now be that big girl I taught you to be and talk to Jen. For Christ's sake, you two live together and you haven't talked in a couple days. That's not healthy for ANY relationship."

"Okay, Mom, I'll do that. Thank you for talking."

"Whoa, Whoa, Whoa! Wait a minute, sit back down, missy. Hope, my dear, you need to listen to Sean and Ray. You have to fix this before you hit rock bottom."

"What's wrong with rock bottom?"

"Well nothing, but once you hit it, who's going to be there to pick you up?"

"You?"

"No, I think I have yoga that day."

"Mom, you are silly. But I get what you're saying. Love you."

"Love you too, sweetie."

I grabbed my purse and headed to the car. Don't get me wrong, things were going great. I mean, I was Kelly's other right-hand man, and the account I'd taken over had given me shitloads of money and I was able to relax and love life, but I missed my gal pal. Kelly had been trying her best to fill that void, but after speaking with my mother, who knows me best, I realized I really was in the wrong and I needed to grow some balls.

When I got home I needed a pick-me-up. I grabbed my phone, plopped on the couch, and checked Bang. Now we were talking some entertainment stuff: more friend requests and messages. The amount of messages I got about babes and sexy and hot face—*I want to lick things off your body* and such—made me gag! I couldn't help but feel icky! I wondered how people could post half-naked pictures and not throw up because of the sickos out there. Bang was starting to get a little boring, and I thought it was maybe ruining me and my life. I don't know; maybe I was just going crazy and Jen-deprived.

* * *

Dear Diary,

I admit I have a Bang problem. I also have a problem with my boss, Kelly. She wants to get extra close and she's having tons of secret phone calls. I miss my Jen and the boys. Tomorrow should be better; I get to hear my Richie's voice. Goodnight.

<3 Clinically Depressed Hope

My Love is Closer

So it had been a couple weeks since I'd seen my love! And—I know, I know—I was all mushy-gushy. I had to admit, this Bang thing hadn't turned out so bad. I'd been dying to get my arms around Richie's gorgeous neck for so long now! Granted, we hadn't had sex, so I was patiently waiting to get my groove on! I'd already bought a sexy outfit for Saturday, aka my b-day, so hopefully I would get some lovin'!

I was cleaning up when something kept vibrating my leg; it had been a while, and I didn't want this feeling to go away. Finally it stopped, and I got two little vibrations after that. Damn it, I'd missed Richie's call! At least he texted me.

"Hey love. You must be bust. I just wanted to let you know I'm back in town and tonight I'm taking my favorite girl out. Be ready by 7, we have dinner and a night of salsa dancing.

I sat on my couch, in total love and admiration for this man. I hadn't felt this kind of love since Hanky, and to think this was possible because of Bang.com. Yes, I'd been totally against it; I even believe I'd kicked and screamed, cried a little also, and I'd tried to plead my case against this stupid site. Since caving into peer pressure, I'd gained a love, had more friends and a bigger network, and I was building my confidence. The only downside, I would have to say, to Bang was that it was really time-consuming and addicting. By the time I got off the phone and realized what time it was, it was five thirty! I heard a long bath calling my name before he came at seven.

Soaking in the tub for about 30 minutes, I allowed myself to be in total solitude. I heard someone at the door but ignored it. I glanced down at my watch; it was only six o'clock, so I knew it wasn't Richie. Jen had a key and the boys always break-and-entered.

I found the knocking to stop, and I slowly drifted to sleep. After maybe 10 minutes of conking out, I felt a presence in the room with me, like there was someone watching over me. I slowly opened my right eye; just in case there was a serial killer on the toilet, I would catch him off guard and attack first.

"Richie?"

"Hello, gorgeous. I know, I'm early. I couldn't stand being away from you for much longer. I also let myself in. You know, you should lock your doors, this isn't the fifties."

He leaned over to give me a kiss and placed my roses on the countertop. I soon heard the front door open.

"Jen?!" I yelled.

"Hey, is Dick here? because there is a car outside that looks just like his!"

"Oh yeah, that Dodge? No, that's Richie's."

"Where is he?"

"In here with me."

"Oh really?!"

"Not like that, you freak."

"Yeah, sure! I love having men in the bathroom with me so we can have in-depth conversations, happens all the time. Well, Richie, maybe I'll meet you someday, just not now, because that would be weird."

"So that's Jen?"

"Yes, that's my girl."

"You guys fixed things yet?"

"No, not yet. She probably just spoke to me because she thought you were Dick."

"Well, whatever the reason, I'm sure it will pass. Now hurry up, we have reservations."

I jumped out of the tub and continued to get ready. I put on minimal makeup and a nice, plain-Jane black dress. Jen stayed in her room to give us space and probably because she didn't want to see my face either.

"Wow, you look amazing."

"Why, thank you. Okay, Jen, I'm out of here!"

I waited for a response but I got nothing. I turned to Richie and his phone was blowing up.

"So many calls and texts tonight, I see."

"Yeah, it's my boss. She can wait."

We got into his car and drove off into the night. We reached a very cool intimate Spanish restaurant that had seating on one side and on the other a nice dance floor lit with dark red bulbs.

"So, Hope, I really like you," Richie said to break the ice.

"I really like you, too."

"I want you to meet my family, but that involves a trip to California."

"I would love to. I want you to meet mine also. We have a family dinner tomorrow in pre-celebration of my birthday, so if you're up for it...?"

"That sounds perfect to me."

For the rest of the night, we talked, drank, ate, and danced the night away. Being in his arms made everything feel so right and comfortable. Tonight was the night I fully trusted another man.

***

Dear Diary,

Becoming a believer Hope

Richie and the Family

Today was the day: Richie, my lover in life, the one I had been so anxiously waiting for, was going to meet my family. I knew I shouldn't and it seemed too fast, but hey, when you know, you know, right?

I woke up in a decent mood and work was oh-so-strange. Surprised? I think not. Kelly was on some random secret phone call again; I would've loved to know what she was up to. She decided to let me leave work early; I had no idea why, but I didn't want to ask. So now I was getting ready for Richie to pick me up so we could go to my parents' house. I was slowly pacing back and forth in the bathroom, getting my thoughts together on tonight and praying to sweet baby Jesus that things would go fine, when the doorbell rang.

"Hey, love bug!"

"Hey there, doll," Richie said as he handed me a bouquet of my fave flowers, aka sunflowers. I smiled and planted a big one on his lips.

"Wow, loving you some Richie today, huh?"

"Of course! Every day, not just today. So are you ready to meet my family?"

"Of course, my love."

"Now, I warn you on how they really are and you promise not to run away?"

"Unless they chase me with a gun or knife I'm right by your side, baby!"

Now I may already have been just head over heels for him. *Lord, oh lord, please let my family behave tonight! Just for one night! Hey, I'm not even asking for the full night, just a couple hours until we leave, then BAM, lay down the random acts! Thank you, sweet baby Jesus.*

"Wow, that was a long car ride!"

"Yeah, it's a good long ten minutes. I like to blame the random railroad tracks in the street that surprisingly have no railroad signs." We both shared a laugh and he locked eyes with me for a good 30 seconds.

"Hope, you are one amazing woman."

We kissed again for about another 10 minutes in the car. I felt like I was in high school, but the only difference was that there was a boy in the car and I wasn't faking this time. Walking up the stairs and to the door, I could already hear the screaming and crying.

"Shut up! I believe they are here! Now let us all be on

our best behavior. God knows I want her to have a man, I need more grandbabies." The door flew open and there she was, my mother, with her apron on and bright pink lipstick. "Oh, Hope! Come on in, darling! Give me a kissy-kiss and some huggy-hugs!" Mom reached for me and held me as tight as she could.

"Ma—" My breath was slowly leaving my body and I began to feel lightheaded. "Maaa— Mom!"

"Oh, sorry, dear! I've been working out. So is this Richie?"

"Yes. Mom this is Richie, Richie this is my mother, Helen."

"Pleasure to meet you, Helen."

"Pleasure to meet you! Oh, come on in, we are all excited to meet you! Hope has told us all about you." We followed Mom into the living room, where I made eye contact with Richie and said, "I'm sorry."

My sister, Lindsey, and brother-in-law, Ryan, were on the couch, being awkward and uncomfortable, arguing like always. My dad had the TV blaring as loud as he could, my nieces and nephews were running around, and my uncle Mike was in the corner listening to his walkman, dancing in a glittery shirt.

"Everyone, Hope is here! And this is her man, Richie! You guys, get up and come say hi!"

Lindsey was the first to get up and walk quickly in our direction. "Hey, s'up."

"Hi," Richie said, looking confused.

"I'm Lindsey, the sista! Bet you heard all about me, huh?" she asked as she fixed her hair.

"Actually no, I haven't."

Lindsey then turned red and her little devil horns began to come out. Before she could rip his head off, he cut her off and said, "Lindsey, nice to meet you, I was joking. Hope told me all about you. You're a fascinating woman as well."

"Oh," Lindsey giggled. "Well I like you already. Will you be coming to her birthday party this Saturday?"

"Of course."

"Good." My sis walked to sit down. Ryan got up to walk to us slowly, making eye contact with his wife.

"Okay, baby, now this is Ryan, Ray, my BFF's, brother," I whispered to him.

"Hey, you must be Ryan? Nice to meet you, you and Lindsey have some beautiful kids."

"Yeah, man, that's just on the outside." Ryan waved

for Richie to come closer. "They are little spawns of Satan. My little girl is the devil herself, does rituals and all that. My sons have a potty mouth and probably already lost their virginity. See their mother on the couch? Don't buy that nice act. I did, and look what happened. I don't have any more balls, man! They are all go—"

"RYAN!" yelled Lindsey.

"Yes, dear, I'm coming."

"See? I told you. Just wait, it gets better," I whispered. I'm glad Richie was taking this lightly, because man, I was sweating bullets.

"HEY, MAN! They call me Uncle Mike! Feel free to do the same. What's your favorite movie?"

"Mine? Well, ummm..."

"Ah, it's *The Shining*, huh?"

"Yeah, it is. How did you know?"

"Because you look like a *Shining* kind of guy, ha!" As Uncle Mike hit Richie's arm harder than a piece of chopped wood, they both shared an awkward laugh. "Hey, princess, I like this cat! He's cool with me."

"Okay, and now this is the man of my life, good ol' Dad, aka Bill!"

"Bill, nice to meet you!"

"Same here. What's your favorite sport?"

"I can't pick a favorite sport, sir, I love them all!"

"AHH! My boy! Welcome to the family!"

Well, it seemed like my love had passed with flying colors. I guessed I could stop sweating and get on to having a relaxed night then, huh?

"Okay, guys, dinner is ready!" yelled Mom. "I hope y'all don't mind, I broke the oven so we are having Thai!"

Oh, sweet baby Jesus, you outdid yourself tonight! Now I could toss the bottle of Pepto I'd brought with me. We all sat at the table, exchanging laughs and stories. The kids were behaving, and my family seemed to be a little normal until my awesome nephew Trey had to ruin it for a little bit.

"So, Richie, have y'all banged yet?"

Everyone stopped talking, Lindsey was going crazy, my dad and Ryan were laughing, and my mom spit out her drink.

"TREY!" yelled Lindsey. "That is totally rude and none of your business!"

"Well, Trey, out of respect for your aunt, no, we haven't," said Richie.

"You're gay," said Albert.

"ALBERT!" yelled my sister.

"How do you figure that?" asked Richie.

"Oh my God, I am so sorry for my children!"

"Because you haven't banged, and Mommy says Daddy's gay because he doesn't bang, either," said Melissa, aka Hissy.

Now this was definitely awkward. I thought it was funny, but I pretended to be appalled because my sister would glare every time I giggled. As the table went into complete chaos, I looked at Richie and smiled, and he gave me a kiss on the forehead. Lindsey was trying to get the kids and avoid eye contact with Ryan.

"Well, 'rents, it's time for us to go!"

"Nice to meet you guys!" Richie said with a smile.

"Oh dear, I'm so sorry, let me walk you guys out." Mom said.

"Helen, it was wonderful. The dinner was great, and I enjoyed every bit of it! Next time I'll cook."

"Lindsey, Ryan, Bill, Uncle Mike, nice to meet all of you. I'll see you Saturday."

We said our goodbyes and drove off into the night.

* * *

Dear Diary

Tonight was great despite the dysfunctional mess of the fam-bam. Everything seems to be falling into place. Now I need to make nice with the friends. That's on my to-do list for tomorrow. Goodnight.

<3 I Knew Everything Would Be Alright Hope

What Just Happened?

I woke up to a frantic text message from Kelly, saying that I needed to be at work an hour early. Good thing Sean made my phone go off every five minutes until I pick it up, otherwise I would've missed the importance of Kelly's Message.

I scrambled to get dressed and jumped into old faithful and sped down the highway to work. I saw only Kelly's car in the parking lot. I had many thoughts running through my head, did she kill the janitor who always forgets to take out her trash? Did she finally decide to blow up this building and planned on killing me with her? I don't know why my mind automatically went to death, but it's Kelly and she could get away with it.

I ran up the stairs and into her office. "Kelly?"

"Oh my god! Hope!" She ran to me and hugged me

"What's wrong?"

"Daddy"

"Kelly! Did you kill him?!"

"What!? Hell no crazy! He is in town and will be here today"

"And?"

"I didn't tell him about the merge"

"Well, it should bring more business right?

"Yes"

"Tell me what the problem is?"

"Well he has to approve all the merges and if he finds out we merged with a Japanese company he will flip!"

"That's right because your dad is a veteran who went coo coo"

"Exactly"

"So what will happen if he finds out you did this?"

"Well without seeing the numbers he will fire me!"

"Kelly don't be dramatic!'

"No dramatics! When he comes in, he will see that our numbers are off. I will have to explain that to him. Then he will see the bank accounts and notice a huge deposit, what do I say about that?"

"Tell him you have things in the works and needed to cut back on a few things, fire people to get our numbers together. By doing so, you were able to save said amount of money which is what he sees as a deposit. Then he will notice you are smart instead of teaming up with the enemy who almost blew his ears off".
"Hope you are a life saver!"

Right when she hugged me the lights turned on and people started to walk into the building. Kelly decided to send out a mass email to let everyone know that the owner would be coming in. Soon you saw people cleaning their desks, vacuuming, and brushing their teeth. You could smell the franticness in the air.

As I sat down in my chair, I saw man walk in with a woman to his right and a big black dude to his left. That must be the one Kelly calls daddy. I looked into Kelly's office and saw her face light up! You can tell she mouthed the word DADDY!

"Oh my gosh! It's so great to see you!"

"Okay enough with the touching"

"Where's Matt?"

"Well daddy we had to let him go?"

"Why is that?"
"Because he has stealing"

"Stealing?"
"Yes supplies, he now has a weird fetish with paper"

"Must be a gay thing, okay good job."

"Let me see the books"

"Okay, HOPE!" she's my assistant "do you have those reports?"

Yes let me grab them" walked to my desk I never seen Kelly so nervous! She was sweating bullets."Okay here you go"

Kelly's dad began to look over the papers and immediately started to take notes. The chick who was with him was on Kelly's computer pulling an excel sheet with the digital numbers.

"There is a gap here" she said in a stuffy voice "we have lots of numbers missing. There is money that seems to be gone and accounts that seems to be missing"

"Honey, when you fired Matt for stealing, did he take money too?"

Stealing? Matt? What did Kelly say in a span of five minutes alone with her dad? I shot her a look and she tried to ignore me

"No daddy he wouldn't steal he's rich already. Taking accounts wouldn't make any sense"

Now I could see Kelly really starting to sweat, something was off. The lady began to print out paper work and files and whatever else she could find that caused red flags.

"How about I look into it, no worries" Kelly said as she peeked at the papers the lady was printing off her desk. What was going on? Kelly's dad paced back and forth looking at the deposits and noticed a HUGE amount into an account that no one uses for the company.

"Kelly, what is this?"

"What's what?"

"This deposit?"

"Oh shit Hope it's happening!" she whispered

"Don't worry you got this! Just make sure you give credit where it's due aka me! Remember I'm supposed to fill in Matt's job"

"Well daddy we got a new account, we merged with the paper company next door and got them to sign a multimillion dollar contract for two years, with a possible renew after."

"Who is this company?"

"We will talk about that later"

"Who got this account? You?"

"Yes"

"Did you get any help, or you pulled this off solo?"

Okay here it is, Kelly is about to tell pops my involvement and I will get Matt's job once and for all! I'm nervous but I started to fix myself up in the mirror as I waited for Kelly to answer.

"Yes, did it all by myself daddy!"

"That's my girl! I knew who were smart somehow!" they hugged and smiled towards one another

"WHAT THE HELL!" I yelled

"Hope are you okay?" asked Kelly's dad

"Hope" Kelly whispered

"I helped, actually I'm the one who got the account for us sir"

"Is this true?"

"No daddy she must be off her medicine I got it.

Hope, Dear, why don't you go to your desk and take those pills, it's about that time."

"Kelly what are you doing?" I mumbled

"I owe you one, sorry but mama needs this!"

As she pushed me out the door I looked back at the office full of executives and screamed "JAPAN!"

"Don't you say that word in here!"

"Daddy calm down it's okay, Hope get out!"

"Kelly merged with a Japanese company despite my efforts of telling her that you don't like the Japanese for respectable reasons."

Kelly stood in her office shocked and eyes filled with tears. "Hope" she let out a very mum breath.

"Is this TRUE!?"

"Yes daddy"

"I see, gather everyone into the conference room and call your brother, we need to have a meeting here in twenty minutes."

Kelly walked to her desk and called Matt as I walked to mine and instructed everyone to meet in the conference room in twenty minutes. The air was thick, it felt sad and angry. Kelly didn't lift her head once when people started to walk in.

"Hello everyone I'm Mr. Sharps. Owner of Sharps INC. It comes to my attention that this place has slowly been on the downfall. My daughter here took it upon herself to fire Matt, make budget cuts and merge with a group of people I don't like. She has displayed poor choices with her short time as leader of this company. I take it upon myself to appoint Matthew Sharps as COO and back in his rightful place."

"DADDY! What about me?"

"Oh Kelly dear, you're fired and cut OFF!"

"DADDY?!"

"OUT! Thanks Hope for helping me realize the true hearts of those on my team, you will be rewarded with something. As for the rest of you, I look forward to our one on ones you are dismissed."

As I walked out the conference room I felt all eyes on me. I couldn't escape the looks of disappointment from everyone at work.

Dear Diary,

Did I really just get Kelly fired and cut off? say it isn't so! The screwed up Hope

The Make-Up

Okay, okay, so I know already! I was a bitch to my BFF and she didn't deserve any of that. Granted, I was the one who flaked and forgot all about our meeting; and yes, I was the one who ignored her calls and texts, and.... Okay I get it! I was the one who pretty much spit on all her ideas because Kelly wanted me to. And yes, now I see that was wrong. I should have had more of my own mind!

Jen and I were pretty much nonexistent and the boys were really mad at me. They went on strike and wouldn't come around or answer my calls or texts until I made nice with Jen. So this morning I took it upon myself to do just that: ask for forgiveness! It was a simple case of WWJD— What Would Jen Do.

"Hey, sexy!" I said, smiling at Jen, who was in the kitchen pigging out on a box of Pops cereal. She didn't respond, just looked up and went right back to reading her magazine.

"I said hey, sexy! What ya got cookin', good lookin'?" And still no response. "So I was thinking, maybe you and I can hit up that new shop downtown, you know, NES Fashions? Chick comes from Alaska, and she is awesome! I loved this black print dress, and it would look fabulous on m—"

"OH, SHUT UP! I get it! Your life is so amazing and you can afford such hot clothes at NES Fashions! Yadda, yadda, yadda! Look, you Kelly-wannabe, bimbo, smart-mouth-havin' ho, I don't care!"

"Okay, so Jen, how did you sleep?"

"Pretty shitty."

"I figured, but hey, look, I was just trying to break the ice and talk about something you like, aka fashion, and I know how much you love Natasha and her designs, so I figured I would grab your attention by going to her store and whatnot. But I see it's not working so I'll just flat out say it. Dude, I'm super sorry for everything."

"Go on."

"And I realize that I was turning into such a bitch and following instead of leading."

"Good job, Athena."

I turned around to see Ray and Sean peeking into our

kitchen window.

"Oh, hey, guys?" I said, being really confused.

"Those freaks have been stalking the windows ever since you were a bitch. They wanted to catch your apology," said Jen.

"So you mean to tell me they have been stalking outside for the past—"

"Yup, five days," said Ray.

"Great," I said.

"Well, now since you are off your high horse, how about we all play hookie and ditch work and go celebrate the reunion of us?" asked Sean.

"That sounds like a splendid idea," replied Ray.

"How are we able to pay our bills? We take off work more than Paris Hilton," I said.

As we all joked and loved on each other for about two minutes, we did just that: got our shit together and started off today as a great make-up session. Shopping, here we come!

"Hey, Hope! Welcome back!" Natasha said as we all entered in NES Fashions.

"Wow, you come here a lot, Athena?"

"A lot? She pretty much lives in here since she changed her style," Jen snipped.

"Well who is that sexy, short little lady?" asked Ray.

"Oh, that's Natasha. She's from Alaska and she owns this boutique."

"Owns a boutique and lives with *Twilight*? Oh, we are destined to be together! Get out of my way! Ray-Ray has to put on the moves."

"He does know that vampires don't exist?" Sean whispered to Jen.

"Maybe, let's not ruin his groove," Jen added.

As Jen and I began to shop for dresses, Ray was busy trying to put "the mack daddy" on Natasha, and Sean was staring at the awkwardly shaped mannequins. So far we were livin' large!

"Hey, so is Richie coming to the party?" Jen asked.

"Yeah, we never met this guy! And you've been dating him for quite some time now, Athena."

"Yes, he will be. I took him to meet the family last week."

"Wow! He met the obnoxious fam-bam? This must be serious!" said Jen.

"It's getting there, all he has to do is meet my closest friends and all will be set!"

"Exciting! So Jen, is your boy toy coming too?"

"No, unfortunately he said he has a meeting out of town and can't make it."

"That sucks, looks like I'll be your date!"

"No, balls-for-brains."

"Why not, slutterella?"

"Because I don't want to be seen with you like that Papa Smurf."

"I love it when you call me big papa!"

"Ugh! Why do I talk to you?"

"I ask myself the same thing. I would rather you stand there bent over, but for some reason you won't."

"Listen here, you little shi—"

"ENOUGH! Look, I found a dress! You two behave while I go try this on!"

Sitting there unwillingly, Jen and Sean sat in awkward silence waiting for me to come out. I'd picked out this black dress with tiger print and some Dolce & Gabbana shoes. All I needed were the right accessories and I would be set.

"Okay! Grab Ray and Natasha, I think this is the right fit!" As Jen and Sean went to go fetch the other two, I was staring in the mirror at the most beautiful woman ever!

"Okay, okay, Athena, come out!"

"Okay, you ready?!"

"No, Sean just likes telling people to come out for

fun," Jen said.

"Shut it. Okay, here I am! Tada!"

I whipped open the curtain, and there I was in the most flawless dress in all of Arizona, and it was on my body! So fitting, with the perfect clutch and shoes.

"Wow, you look amazing!" said Natasha. "I have some accessories that would go great with this!"

As Natasha went to go grab the accessories, my friends sat in awe and Jen tried not to cry.

"Look at my little dirt-under-the-fingernails-having princess! She is all grown up! And I didn't even have to help pick this out!" And then the waterworks began.

"Thanks, Jen. So, boys, what do you think?"

"Man, you look hot, Athena! In that dress you can run my mother ship anytime!"

"Yeah, what brains said," said Ray.

I smiled, knowing I'd done well, and placed the jewelry on that Natasha had gone to grab for me—a long gold chain and some bracelets. I had Natasha take a picture of me so I could send it to Richie.

"So Hope! What's new in the cut throat industry of Sharps?" asked Jen

"Meh not much"

"Lies!" said Ray

"Yeah Athena, spill the beans"

"Well Matt is back as COO, Mr.Sharps came in and cleaned the place"

"Like literally?" asked Sean

"Yeah like mop and bucket" smiled Jen

"Like me getting Kelly fired. SO what about that dress!"

"WHAT! NO get back here!" said Ray

"You got Cruela Daville fired?"

"Yes Jen"

"How?!" said Sean with his eyes wide open

"Long story short, her dad was in the war almost got killed by the Japanese and the company we merged with is Japanese. She didn't give me credit and tried to talk to me as if I were a three year old. So I got mad and---"

"and you snitched on her because you got your feelings hurt?" asked Ray

"Kinda"

"Kinda? Athena! Not cool! Okay later on when pops wasn't around you two could've hashed that out. I mean you had to know he would do something that drastic!"

"Yeah she mentioned that"

"And yet you still said that?" asked Jen "Oh Hope that's bad karma"

Some Quality Time with Friends

Today was FRIDAY! Want to know why I was super excited? Well, my birthday is TOMORROW and we were planning the most EPIC birthday bash I'd ever had. Granted, my previous birthday consisted of Chunky Monkey ice cream and the movies *Grease* and *Flash Dance*, followed by an orchestra of tears for the disaster that had come, but it had still been a good day. TOMORROW, however, would be the best! I had my lovely boyfriend coming, my family and friends, who honestly had been kinda rude lately, and some more people.

It was already one o'clock; where were my buds? Soon the doorbell rang and I rushed to the door.

"LIKE, O! M! G! HI, GUYS!" They sat there, stared at each other, and then slowly entered the house.

"See, Jen created this monster—the makeover, the everything, the social networking.... She is a beast! A scary one," whispered Sean to Ray.

"Yeah, and now we are stuck with her," said Ray.

I turned around fast and hugged my two handsome men. "SOOO! Jen is out getting us some booze, so let's talk, catch up, it's been like a million years!"

"Yeah, catch up," said Sean. "What's up with your voice? Catch us up on that."

"Whoa! Do I sense some 'tudage?"

"No, he's right, what's up with your voice? You sound like Kelly."

"Yeah, well, after we became friends on Bang we are inseparable."

"Inseparable? Hope, you got her fired," said Sean.

"No I didn't!"

"Really, Hope? Sean is right, you got her fired and you guys are still close. Is she coming tomorrow?"

"Yes, she is. And okay, first and foremost, I did not get her fired. She just failed to show up during the meeting with the CEO and President."

"And why did she NOT show up?" asked Ray.

"Because…"

"Because YOU made sure her car wouldn't start so you would look really good in the meeting," blurted Sean.

"Okay, whatever!"

Under a lot of heat, I heard something scratching at the door. I took a peek outside and saw that Jen was home with arms full of groceries. Boy, I had NEVER been more excited to see her. I ran to the door and helped her out. She was NOT in a great mood today. She'd planned to show off her boyfriend, Richard, to us all tomorrow at my birthday. We were all trying to get her mind of off it, so today was a Jen day: time for talks and movies, followed by lots of liquor. Jen started to vent on how much of an ass Richard was. She said that he'd dumped her and the reason was that he'd found a new hottie. They'd dated for quite a long time, and the fact that she was JUST about to introduce him to us let us know she actually liked him. We had a successful intervention with Jen about how she'd let herself go. They tried to speak to me about myself, but HELLO! I was NOT about to let that happen!

Well, my new BF's name was Richie; I hoped Jen didn't cry or get too mad when I introduced them tomorrow, since they had the same name. Anything that started with an R made Jen furious. No watching *Ren and Stimpy*, no watching *The Amazing Race* or even saying, "I'm going for a run." Any R-word was out of the question for now. Yes, she was going through something deep. My heart broke for her.

"So tell me what happened?"

"We were going so good! Then all of a sudden he got busy and wouldn't take my calls. He would always text me but never speak to me. No face chat no nothing! The when we were together he keeps getting messages from another woman and he would dodge my questions! I think I'm being to paranoid."

"No honey you are being the right amount. Have you talked to him latetly?"

"Yeah I invited him to your birthday"

"Seriously? No drama at the pizarty!"

"There won't be I'll make sure of that I just want you to check him out for me"

"Deal, now what do you want to watch?"

"Saw"

"You're such a lady!"

* * *

Dear Diary,

What the hell am I doing?

<3 Hope

It's MY BIRTHDAY!

Alright! Today was the day! It was my birthday! I know I shouldn't have been that excited since I was getting deeper and deeper into my 30s. Soon I'd be 100 and then I would die. This birthday was amazing! Not only because I had a great BF, but my friends and my family were coming and I looked damn good! I ran over the preparations with Jen one more time before we started to set up. For some reason she was being a sourpuss. She needed to get over that because it was my birthday and it was my damn day.

"Hey, Jen."

"Hi."

"So let's get to decorating! Here is the list and I will be right back."

"Wait, where are you going?"

"Well I have a nail appointment, then I have to get my hair did!"

"So you want me to do all this while you get all Barbied up?"

"Um, yeah!"

"Well tough shit, this is YOUR birthday! We do this TOGETHER or not at all!"

"Well, Jen, I believe you're just jealous."

"Of what, bleach head?"

"Of me and my bleached head."

"Oh, HA! Yeah the frick right! How about you take that tissue outta your shirt, put on some big girl pants, and take care of your shit."

"OR you, my little oily faced minion, can do that for me."

For some reason Jen didn't even fight back. I would

have thought she'd have had some fire in her. I guess not.
Instead she picked up her purse and left the house. Great!
Now because of a selfish person I would have to do this all
by myself. I called the salon to push back my appointment
and got started on my decorations. I blew up balloons, draped
streamers, pulled out the decorative table cloths, set out the
chips, plates, cups, the usual, and then hopped in the shower
and headed over to the salon. That had taken way longer than
I expected! I knew it would be worth it, though.

After I dished it out with the ladies at the salon, I was
officially sexy and it was time to enjoy this party! I decided
to go with the bubblegum dress that Jen had picked out for
me when we did the makeover, and let me tell you—I don't
mean to toot my own horn, but TOOT, TOOT! I was sex-ay!
Soon people started to arrive: first the DJ, who set up in the
living room; then my family. Ray, Sean, and Jen came right
after. After that were my coworkers, some online friends, and
my boyfriend.

The music was going, and people were dancing and
having fun. I was the perfect socialite of the evening. I
looked over to Jen, who seemed to see a ghost, as I headed
over to Kelly and Richie to see what they were talking about.
Richie was over by Kelly and some weirdos, laughing and
pointing towards Jen, Sean, and Ray, who weren't more than

five feet apart. I felt an odd vibe, so I decided to see what was up.

"Hey, babe."

"Hey, you," I said. "So what ya'll talking about?"

"Well, Kelly pointed out how gross Jen is. I agree, she does look like a washed-up Marilyn Monroe. Can't believe I dated her!"

"Dated who?"

"Jen."

"When did that happen?

"Well, it was short-lived, but it's over now."

Putting two and two together, I realized my Richie was Jen's ex, Richard, who'd JUST dumped her about two weeks ago. Come to think of it, he and I had been going for almost a month, and if he'd just dumped her, that meant he'd cheated on me.

"Babe, don't ruin the party, Listen, I mean, come on, it's your birthday. She could've at least straightened up a little. And then the big bag of muscles always looks so uptight and I have no idea why. It's like he's pissed that he can't reach around and wipe his own ass. Now as for Akbar over there, I don't know if he's gonna bomb us or par-tay!"

I was in total shock. The words he spoke were ridiculous, and Kelly was laughing. Their whole circle was laughing. Jen and them weren't too pleased, one bit. They looked at me to shut him up, and there I was, torn between two things. One, my friends, and two, this guy who, despite his mouth at the moment, could be the real deal. I put on a smile and headed over to Richie, grabbed his arm tight, and continued to talk. I noticed my parents drop their heads in shame.

"So that's Richie huh? No wonder the car looked familiar"

"Jen I had no idea I mean I--"

"Dude it's okay, he's a player. Besides we are broken up...again.... Remember?"

I looked at Jen who was obviously trying to fight back some tears.

"Yo that dude is a straight dick Hope! And you're gonna let him stay?" snapped Sean

"I mean he is my boyfriend"

"right, yours and Jens and probably Kelly's too" said Ray

"Kelly's? No definitely not"

"Are you sure?" Ray said as he point over to Kelly who was really close to her "cousin". She had her arm intertwined with his and when she laughed she would rest her head on his shoulder

227

"Not sure about you, but I don't touch my cousins like that" said Sean

"Hmm maybe it's a southern thing" said Ray

"Yeah that would be believable but he's from New York" said Jen

"I'll be back" I walked over to Richie and Kelly to see what they were talking about. Of course it was nothing major, just complaints on my party and it's appearance.

"Who wants cake?!" yelled my mom trying to lighten the mood. As she brought out the cake everyone was singing and I was looking around. Things started to piece themselves together. Richie was the one I saw on Kelly's page, Richie is in fact Jens boy friend. Something just didn't feel right and little did I know things were about to get worse.

"Can I have your attention everyone!" Kelly yelled as she hit a knife on the side of her glass "Okay so today is our dear Hopes' birthday. I prepare a little slideshow with some audio and video just for you Hope." Kelly looked over to Riche to cue up the slide show "Who would've thought that our Hope would turn into this woman that she is now." On the screen was a picture of me in my old clothes and fat pockets everywhere. "She was once this little acne covered, coke bottle glasses freak. Skin so pale and nails were just horrible. One day after she broke up with her turd of a man she decided to change herself. You would think one would be appreciative of hose who helped her get to where she is now. Jen, her "bff"" as Kelly put it into quotations "was the main one who stood by her friends side, like a true champion." Then the slide changed to a picture of Kelly and I in the nail salon "For some reason Hope could careless" Kelly looked over to Riche who hit the play button on some audio. Soon the entire room heard my rants on my friends. Me making fun of Jen and talking bad about my circle. MY eyes started to fill with tears as I watched Jen break down and Ray consoling her. Soon a video was shown of me mocking those I work with. As soon as the part came on where I was making fun of Matt Sharps new owner, he walked into the room. I walked over to Kelly and tried to grab the remote from her hands

"What are you doing?" I whispered

"Not so fun anymore huh? Shouldn't have tried to undermine me; OH yeah not to mention getting me fired"

"I think we've see enough" said Matt as he walked over and too control of the situation. He stood in the middle of Kelly and I as he had the projector shut down. "We all make mistakes, it's unfortunate that Hope has made these ones. It also sucks that she thought she could trust and confide in such an evil soul like my sister. Kelly this was not the place nor time to do this. We could've had a sit down just us three"

"Awe broham, then what pleasure would I get from watching her cry?"

"Kelly you will never work or own anything that has to do with Sharps again. As for you Hope, two weeks from now will be your last day. I'm getting rid of all the poison in my business."

As everyone slowly walked out of my party, Jen was so hurt she couldn't even speak to me. I tried to apologize to everyone as they were walking out but no one was having it.

"Hey Hope, happy birthday dear" Kelly smiled grabbed Richie and walked out.

The End of a Monster

I laid in my bed, not wanting to move or talk to anyone...not that people were talking to me at the moment. I got up slowly, staring at that damn cat who hated me, too; he wouldn't even make a noise. Great, now Garfield was giving me the silent treatment, too. I walked towards the bathroom, passing what used to be Jen's room. I looked in the mirror and saw someone I didn't know. My face was caked with running mascara; red, smeared lipstick; and baby blue eye shadow. My hair was frizzy and a complete mess, while my shirt was halfway ripped, and my bra strap was falling off my right shoulder. Last night had been a night I did not wish on anyone.

I managed to pull myself together and jump in the shower. I had to go to work today and give a big presentation to the boss on why I should be considered for VP of our company. I turned the water on hot, stared at my shampoo bottle, and began to cry. I fully realized I'd lost myself, my true goals, my friends, and possible my family. It was supposed to be my birthday weekend, but instead I'd turned it into *Jerry Springer* with a dash of *The Wendy Williams Show*. Jumping out of the shower, I put on some natural-looking makeup and a black suit with a powder pink button-

231

up shirt and headed to work. The entire car ride, I couldn't help but hold back tears and memorize my speech.

Pulling into the crowded parking lot, I managed to squeeze my 1996 VW Beetle between two pickup trucks. Grabbing my briefcase, coffee, and brain, I ran into work, bypassing the receptionist, and into the meeting room. I started to set up my laptop and hook it up to the projector screen. The CEO came in, greeted me, and sat down so sternly I almost peed myself. *Come on, Hope, let's get this together. Show the man what you're working with.*

"Good morning, Mr. Stands," The jerk nodded. Not even a smile, just a head nod. "I'm glad you could make it, let's get to the presentation, shall we. We all know that I love this company. I have been here for over five years now. I've watched it grow, I've seen people break apart when we didn't meet quota, and I've stood above the rest, picking up the pieces and carefully putting them back together. Now, as I start up the PowerPoint, we will go into a mini presentation of my statistics here, and how, since I've been with this company, we have profited over three times the amount of revenue." I reached down and noticed I didn't have my thumb drive. *SHIT! Okay, do not panic, Hope, play it smooth. Nothing is worse than someone being unprepared and then panicking. Make something up and make it good!*

"I do apologize, Mr. Stands, let us take a mini restroom break before I get too deep."

"That is a great idea! I had a huge cup of coffee. I would hate to excuse myself while you are presenting."

So we took a break. I ran like I'd just committed a murder to my desk. Turning the corner, I was shocked by what I saw. It was Jen, Ray, and Sean, sitting right there at my desk. I couldn't believe they were here, and I couldn't help but wonder why. I walked slowly, fighting tears but trying to keep it safe and sane.

"Hey," I said.

"S'up, Athena?" asked Sean. He was the vocal one; Jen didn't look at me too much, and Ray just nodded.

"What are you doing here?"

"Well, we know you are aware that you were a total bitch to us. You tried to sabotage our relationship, and for what? Someone you met? That sucks and shows us how you can really be," said Sean.

"On top of that, you allowed it to happen. You didn't stick up for your friends. You didn't even kick him out. Instead you smiled, laughed, flipped your hair, and walked away," commented Ray.

"Not to mention, you were a bitch," said Jen.

Standing there, looking at them, I saw my support

system hurting, and I was the one who'd done it. The people who loved me in my time of need, the ones who picked me up and stood by my side, were right in front of my face at my job, despite what I'd done.

"Guys, I am so sorry. I did not mean to do it, and I promise it won't happen again."

"Yeah, we know. We love the old Hope, the one not so up to technology," said Sean.

"Th girl who hated make up and push-up bras" said Jen.

"And the one who would speak for us when we couldn't even find the words," said Ray.

"That's the Hope that we miss," Sean said as he turned my chair to face the computer. "So we are doing this because we love you."

"What are you doing?"

"We are deactivating your account. Some people aren't meant for social networking," Ray replied.

I sat in awe, watching them delete my account. They loved me this much that they'd still come, they were still here to pick up the pieces I'd dropped.

"Now, I believe you are looking for this." Jen whipped out my thumb drive.

"How did you know?"

"Well, as I packed, I accidentally took it. Which is what brought us here in the first place."

"Yeah, she was gonna beat your ass, and we came for muscle," said Sean.

"'We?'" I asked.

"Okay! Well Ray is the muscle, I can dial nine-one-one pretty fast."

"Now take that and go kill him in that meeting." Ray smiled.

We all laughed. They hugged me and said they loved me, but if I ever pulled something like that again, we were done! For at least a couple weeks. We all know they cannot live without Hope.

Sometimes we all want love, whether it's fictional or not. We females look at these magazines and think that we have to be as thin as Jen, have great hair like Eva's, a body like Mel's, or a smile like Halley's. But honestly, it's all overrated. Thin is not in; the average American woman is now a size 16, not a size negative two. Yes, the models on TV look amazing and they seem to have it all. For all we know, they could be a total mess, have major issues, but no one will care to ask because they are beautiful. I'd tried to change myself to fit the eyes of my family, friends, coworkers and social media weirdos. I must say, I had fun.

235

My crazy boss deserved what she got, my ex did me so wrong it turned me right, and I gained awesome friends because of him. I guess it's true what they say: it will all work out if you allow God to handle it.

Thanks, Big Guy aka God .

<3 Hope

www.ingramcontent.com/pod-product-compliance
Lightning Source LLC
Chambersburg PA
CBHW031832090426
42741CB00005B/213